Michael M. Dediu, Ph. D.

APHORISMS
AND
QUOTATIONS
With examples and explanations
For everyone

To His Excellency
Mr. H.Th.J.E. Gieskes
The Consul of the Netherlands,
with my best wishes.
The Author

Dedham
April 29, 2012

Library of Congress Cataloging in Publication Data

Dediu, Michael M.

Aphorisms and Quotations

ISBN-13 978-1470113889
ISBN-1470113880

Preface

Aphorisms and quotations are essential for the nourishment of our intellect and for an elevated and civilized life.

This book is based on my collection, for many years, of aphorisms and quotations, and it was a great pleasure to select a few of them to be included here.

For easy reading, I divided the book in two parts:

Part I contains aphorisms and quotations displayed in English first, followed by their Latin or other languages translations and examples.

Part II contains only aphorisms in Latin and other languages, followed by their English translation and examples. Each Part has 10 Chapters, in which I grouped the aphorisms and quotations by topics.

My wife and I included several photos taken in Rome, Italy, to show some the places where many of the mentioned Latin aphorisms and quotations were mentioned or written first, about 2000 years ago.

I want to thank my wife Sophia for her continuous help given to me in writing this book.

We do hope that our readers will enjoy this book, refreshing their wording power, and, ultimately, feeling much better off after finishing it.

We wish all our distinguished readers good reading and great success in using and following these aphorisms and quotations daily, for a better quality of life.

Michael M. Dediu

Table of Contents

PART I English

Chapter I. 1 – Philosophy

A somebody in general, a nobody in particular - Aliquis in omnibus, nullus in singulis
For somebody who knows many general things, but is no expert in anything.
Example: "John read several books, but he is still aliquis in omnibus, nullus in singulis."

A vice is nourished by being concealed - Alitur vitium vivitque tegendo
    Example: "In a company it is better to report corruption, immorality and other vices, otherwise alitur vitium vivitque tegendo."

A word is sufficient for a wise man - Verbum sat sapienti
    Example: "In many critical situations, only one proper word can make the difference between a good or bad output, but it is very difficult to find somebody who knows that proper word, for this we say verbum sat sapienti."

Ad praesens ova cras pullis sunt meliora - Eggs today are better than chickens tomorrow
    Example: "If we have a crisis now, then ad praesens ova cras pullis sunt meliora."

All things change, and we change with them - Omnia mutantur nos et mutamur in illis
    Example: "The life quickly teaches us that omnia mutantur nos et mutamur in illis."

An angry lover tells himself many lies - Amans iratus multa mentitur sibi

    Example: "John loves Mary, but they had a small conflict, and John began to say many strange things; then I told him amans iratus multa mentitur sibi."

As you sow, so shall you reap - Ut sementem feceris ita metes

    Example: "It is very important to teach the children that ut sementem feceris ita metes."

Balzac: Love may be or it may not, but where it is, it ought to reveal itself in its immensity. (Honoré de Balzac)

Balzac: Nobody loves a woman because she is handsome or ugly, stupid or intelligent. We love because we love.

Balzac: Solitude is fine, but you need someone to tell you that solitude is fine.

Balzac: The heart of a mother is a deep abyss at the bottom of which you will always find forgiveness.

Balzac: True love is eternal, infinite, and always like itself. It is equal and pure, without violent demonstrations: it is seen with white hairs and is always young in the heart.

Balzac: What is art? Nature concentrated.

Behold the man - Ecce homo
  Example: "There are many religious paintings and sculptures with the title ecce homo."

Be patient and tough; someday this pain will be useful to you - Perfer et obdura; dolor hic tibi proderit olim
  Example: "There are many painful experiences in life, but perfer et obdura; dolor hic tibi proderit olim."

Buddha: In a controversy, the instant we feel anger; we have already ceased striving for the truth, and have begun striving for ourselves.

Byron: Friendship may, and often does, grow into love, but love never subsides into friendship. (Lord Byron - British Poet)

Byron: Man's love is of man's life a part; it is a woman's whole existence.

Byron: Men love in haste, but they detest at leisure.

Byron: If I don't write to empty my mind, I go mad.
Byron: There is no instinct like that of the heart.

Cutting off an infinite part - Abscisio infiniti
This expression is used when a long speech or explanation must be stopped.

Example: when somebody is talking ad infinitum, kindly suggest: "Nice talk, but please use the abscisio infiniti."

Dediu: Arrogance and self-importance are everywhere, modesty is a rara avis (rare bird).

Dediu: In life try to help yourself, your family, your friends and others. When you cannot help much, just do not create problems.

Dediu: It is very easy to be pessimist; choose the difficult one, and be optimist.

Dediu: Loyalty comes from intense liking and appreciation.

Dediu: Money is a part of happiness, but not the most important.

Deeds, not words - Facta non verba
    Example: "Many times we notice that people, especially politicians and salesmen, promise a lot, but do not deliver;
then let's tell them facta non verba!"

Do not take as gold everything that shines like gold – Non teneas aurum totum quod splendet ut aurum
    Example: "Shakespeare's "All that glitters is not gold" remind us of non teneas aurum totum quod splendet ut aurum."

[Do] to another as [you do] to yourself - Alteri sic tibi
    Example: "In a civilized society, everybody should act thinking first that alteri sic tibi."

Epicurus: It is not so much our friends' help that helps us, as the confidence of their help.

Epicurus: Not what we have, but what we enjoy, constitutes our abundance.

Epicurus: Nothing is enough for the man to whom enough is too little.

Epicurus: Of all the things which wisdom provides to make us entirely happy, much the greatest is the possession of friendship.

Everything happens for a reason - Omnia causa fiunt

   Example: "An important part of our research work, knowing that omnia causa fiunt, is to find causa (the reason)."

Franklin: Your net worth to the world is usually determined by what remains after your bad habits are subtracted from your good ones. (Benjamin Franklin)

Goethe: All intelligent thoughts have already been thought; what is necessary is only to try to think them again. (Johann Wolfgang von Goethe)

Guilty mind - Mens rea

Example: "Many bad things happen because of this mens rea."

He conquers who conquers himself - Vincit qui se vincit
Example: "One, who has a strong auto-control and self-discipline, has a better chance to achive great results, therefore vincit qui se vincit."

He lives twice who lives well- Bis vivit qui bene vivit
Example: "One, who lives well from all points of view, will easily notice that bis vivit qui bene vivit."

Horace: He, who feared he would not succeed, sat still - Sedit qui timuit ne non succederet
Example: "In order to succeed one needs to be very active and motivated, otherwise we apply this: sedit qui timuit ne non succederet."

Horace: Alas! The fleeting years are passing - Eheu! fugaces labuntur anni
Example: "After a number of years, everybody will nostalgically say like Horace: Eheu! fugaces labuntur anni!"

Horace: In peace, as a wise man, he appropriately prepares for war - In pace, ut sapiens, aptarit idonea bello
Example: "It is very unfortunate, but, if we look what happens in the world, we must agree with Horace: in pace, ut sapiens, aptarit idonea bello."

Horace: A picture is a poem without words.

Horace: Words will not fail when the matter is well considered.

Horace: Adversity reveals genius, prosperity conceals it.

Horace: Remember when life's path is steep to keep your mind even.

Horace: No poems can please for long, or live, that are written by water drinkers.

Horace: In laboring to be concise, I become obscure.

Horace: Fortune makes a fool of those it favors too much.

Hunger sweetens the beans - Fabas indulcet fames
    Example: "Peter did not like much the beans, but after some dire experiences, he was very hungry and noticed that fabas indulcet fames."

If you wish for peace, prepare for war - Sic vis pacem para bellum
    Example: "It is very unfortunate, indeed, but the history always proved it, therefore everybody should understand that sic vis pacem para bellum."

In wine there is truth - In vino veritas
    Example: "Drinking some wine gives more willingness to say the truth, therefore we can say in vino veritas"

It is a wise man who speaks little - Vir sapit qui pauca loquitur
    Example: "Somebody, who can use just a few words to describe a complex situation, is very capable, therefore vir sapit qui pauca loquitur."

It is human nature to hate a person whom you have injured - Proprium humani ingenii est odisse quem laeseris
    Example: "It is not good at all, and it should be corrected, but proprium humani ingenii est odisse quem laeseris."

It is not goodness to be better than the worst - Bonitas non est pessimis esse meliorem
Example: "When Sam told his father that he is not the worst in his class, the father told him that bonitas non est pessimis esse meliorem."

It will not always be summer (be prepared for hard times) - Non semper erit aestas
Example: "Be ready for difficult times, because non semper erit aestas."

Know thyself - Nosce te ipsum
Example: "Before you want to know many other things, nosce te ipsum."

Let justice be done through the heavens fall - Fiat justitia ruat caelum
Example: "It is important to have justice for all, and if someone asks to be excepted, the response should be fiat justitia ruat caelum."

Life is not being alive but being well - Vita non est vivere sed valere vita est
Example: "A meaningful life is, certainly, more than merely staying alive, therefore vita non est vivere sed valere vita est."

Life is not being alive but being well - Non est vivere sed valere vita est

 Example: "It is not sufficient to just be alive, you have to be well and do many other things, therefore non est vivere sed valere vita est."

Look back, look at the present, look ahead - Respice, adspice, prospice

 Example: "The definition of history as being like a lamp from the past, turned on in the present, to light the future, was inspired by respice, adspice, prospice."

May he live and flourish for many years - Qui vivat atque floreat ad plurimos annos

 Example: "In addition to "Happy Birthday!" we can say qui vivat atque floreat ad plurimos annos."

Much in little - Multum in parvo

 Example: "This multum in parvo is often used under the acronym form MIP, and it appears for example in computer technology as mipmaps, which need more space in memory."

Mutantur omnia nos et mutamur in illis - All things change, and we change with them

 Example: "With the passing of the years, we begin to notice that mutantur omnia nos et mutamur in illis." - Omnia mutantur, nihil interit

No one gives what he does not have - Nemo dat quod non habet

 Example: "When somebody tries to sell or give something which he does not possess, he should be advised that nemo dat quod non habet."

No one is free who is a slave to his body - Nemo liber est qui corpori servit

Example: "Those who are obsessed with taking care only of their bodies, not of their intellect, will shortly discover the truth that nemo liber est qui corpori servit."

Not anything in excess - Ne quid nimis
Example: "One of the fundamental rules of a good life is ne quid nimis."

Ovid: All things can corrupt when minds are prone to evil

Ovid: All things change, nothing perishes - Omnia mutantur, nihil interit
Example: "Looking carefully around, one can easily observe that omnia mutantur, nihil interit."

Ovid: Art lies by its own artifice.

Ovid: Blemishes are hid by night and every fault forgiven; darkness makes any woman fair.

Ovid: Enhance and intensify one's vision of that synthesis of truth and beauty, which is the highest and deepest reality.

Ovid: Envy aims very high.

Ovid: He who can believe himself well, will be well.

Ovid: In an easy matter, anybody can be eloquent.

Ovid: Love is a credulous thing.

Ovid: Nothing is more powerful than custom or habit.

Ovid: My hopes are not always realized, but I always hope.

Ovid: The first appearance deceives many.

Ovid: The habits change into character.

Ovid: The man who has experienced shipwreck shudders even at a calm sea.

Ovid: Those things that nature denied to human sight, it revealed to the eyes of the soul.

Ovid: The sharp thorn often produces delicate roses.
Ovid: What is now reason was formerly impulse or instinct.

Ovid: Where belief is painful we are slow to believe.

Plato: Any man may easily do harm, but not every man can do good to another.

Plato: Every heart sings a song, incomplete, until another heart whispers back.

Plato: He who is of calm and happy nature will hardly feel the pressure of age, but to him, who is of an opposite disposition, youth and age are equally a burden.

Plato: How can you prove whether at this moment we are sleeping, and all our thoughts are a dream; or whether we are awake, and talking to one another in the waking state?

Plato: The human behavior flows from three main sources: desire, emotion, and knowledge.

Plato: I exhort you also to take part in the great combat, which is the combat of life, and greater than every other earthly conflict.

Plato: It is right to give every man his due.

Plato: The courage is a kind of salvation.

Plato: The excessive increase of anything causes a reaction in the opposite direction.

Plato: The good is the beautiful.

Plato: The man - a being in search of meaning.

Plato: The philosophy begins in wonder.

Plato: The philosophy is the highest music.

Plato: The truth is the beginning of every good to the gods, and of every good to man.

Plato: There are three classes of men; lovers of wisdom, lovers of honor, and lovers of gain.

Plato: There are two things a person should never be angry at, what they can help, and what they cannot.

Plato: There's a victory, and defeat; the first and best of victories, the lowest and worst of defeats which each man gains or sustains at the hands not of another, but of himself.

Plato: Thinking: is the talking of the soul with itself.
Plato: Those who wish to sing always find a song.

Plato: Those who intend on becoming great should love neither themselves nor their own things, but only what is just, whether it happens to be done by themselves or others.

Plato: To prefer evil to good is not in the human nature; and when a man is compelled to choose one of two evils, no one will choose the greater when he might have the less.

Plato: The virtue is relative to the actions and ages of each of us in all that we do.
Plato: The wonder is the feeling of the philosopher, and philosophy begins in wonder.

Plato: We can easily forgive a child who is afraid of the dark; the real tragedy of life is when men are afraid of the light.

Plato: When men speak ill of thee, live so as nobody may believe them.

Plato: When the mind is thinking, it is talking to itself.

Pythagoras: A thought is an idea in transit.

Pythagoras: Do not talk a little on many subjects, but much on a few.

Pythagoras: The oldest, shortest words - "yes" and "no" - are those which require the most thought.

Pythagoras: Silence is better than unmeaning words.

Quintilianus: A liar needs a good memory- Mendacem memorem esse oportet
   Example: "In politics, especially, where the lies are not unusual, it is easy to observe that mendacem memorem esse oportet."

Remember that you will die - Memento mori
   Example: "There are some people who feel so powerful and dominant forever that it is good to be reminded this simple truth: memento mori."

Rousseau: Childhood is the sleep of reason. (Jean-Jacques Rousseau - Philosopher)

Rousseau: Falsehood has an infinity of combinations, but truth has only one mode of being.

Rousseau: It is too difficult to think nobly when one thinks only of earning a living.

Seneca: We all have power to do harm - Ad nocendum patentes sumus

Example: "Even if ad nocendum patentes sumus, we should always try not to do harm."

Seneca: The appearances of things are deceptive and the hope of men is deceived - Fallaces sunt rerum species et hominum spes fallunt

Example: "So frequently, unfortunately, especially in astronomy, what we see is not what we hoped, and we have to repeat after Seneca: fallaces sunt rerum species et hominum spes fallunt."

Small things occupy light minds - Parva leves capiunt animas

Example: "The difficult problems in the world occupy the minds of great people, and parva leves capiunt animas."

Sometimes even the good Homer sleeps - Aliquando bonus dormitat Homerus

It is used to express forgiveness of a work which is not very good.

Example: "This book is good, but the last chapter, well, aliquando bonus dormitat Homerus"

Terence: Lovers are lunatics - Amantes sunt amentes
Example: "Love creates a lot of exuberance, and we can jokingly say that amantes sunt amentes."

Terence: The anger of lovers is the renewal of love - Amantium irae amoris integratio est
Example: "Seeing Ron and July having a little dispute, I reminded them that amantium irae amoris integratio est."

The deepest rivers flow with the least sound - Altissima quaeque flumina minimo sono labiuntur
Example: "In this discussion in a group of people, that professor is much quieter than the others around, because altissima quaeque flumina minimo sono labiuntur"

The root of evil is greed - Radix malorum est cupiditas
Example: "Money itself is a necessity, and, of course it is not evil, but for avarice and greed we can say radix malorum est cupiditas."

The smallest things are most important - Minima maxima sunt
Example: "In life, let's not forget, minima maxima sunt."

The truth shall set you free - Veritas vos liberabit
Example: "Those who lie too much become the prisoniers of their own lies, and they should be reminded that veritas vos liberabit."

The voice of the people is the voice of God - Vox populi vox dei

Example: "Even when the people are oppressed by brutal dictators, after some time, the voice of the people will be heard, because vox populi vox dei."

To err is human, to persevere is of the devil - Errare humanum est, perseverare diabolicum
Example: "Now and then, the parents have to remind their children that errare humanum est, perseverare diabolicum."

There is danger in delay - Periculum in mora
Example: "Especially in the justice system, but also in general, periculum in mora."

Thus passes away earthly glory - Sic transit gloria mundi
Example: "Many oppressive and violent dictators were finally taken out, and then the eliberated people could say sic transit gloria mundi."

To the thresholds of the apostles - Ad Limina Apostolorum
This is an ecclesiastical expression meaning a pilgrimage to the tombs of the Apostles St. Peter and St. Paul at Rome, Italy.

Example: "When we'll go to Rome, let's visit, like the bishops, Limina Apostolorum."

Virgil: Oh, suffering ones, God will grant an end to these things too - O passi gravoria, dabit deus his quoque finem
 Example: "Seeing the consequences of an earthquake, an old man said o passi gravoria, dabit deus his quoque finem."

Virgil: The mind drives matter
 Example: "Many changes around us were produced as result of some initial ideas and plans, therefore mens agitat molem". - Mens agitat molem

Virgil: The woman is always a changeable and capricious thing - Varium et mutabile semper femina
 Example: "Giuseppe Verdi in "La donna e mobile", from his opera Rigoletto, uses this Virgil's comment varium et mutabile semper femina."

Voltaire: Common sense is not so common

Voltaire: We must cultivate our own garden. When man was put in the Garden of Eden he was put there so that he should work, which proves that man was not born to rest.

Who will watch the watchers themselves? - Quis custodiet ipsos custodes?
 Example: "Sometimes we have so many regulators, guards, inspectors and warchers all around us, that we have to ask quis custodiet ipsos custodes?

With the necessary changes - Mutatis mutandis
 Example: "The current situation, mutatis mutandis, can become much better for all."

Wise men love, others are mere lechers - Amabit sapiens, cupient caeteri

    Example: "Analyzing history, it is easy to observe that amabit sapiens, cupient caeteri."

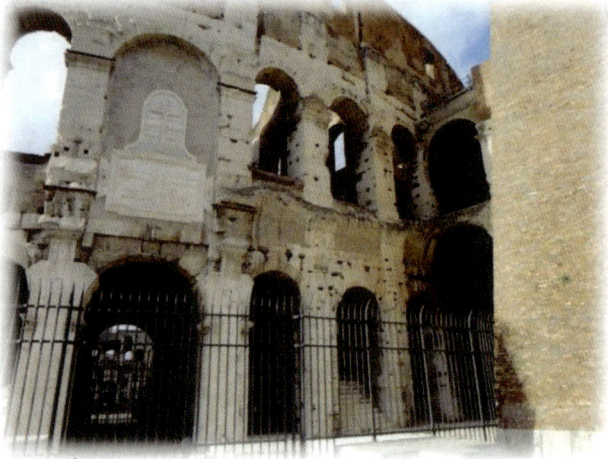

Chapter I. 2 – Success

A mode of living - Modus vivendi
  Example: "A very important issue in life is to find modus vivendi."

Balzac: It is easy to sit up and take notice; what is difficult is getting up and taking action. (Honoré de Balzac)

Balzac: There is no such thing as a great talent without great will power. (Honoré de Balzac)

Balzac: Those who spend too fast never grow rich. (Honoré de Balzac)

Balzac: We exaggerate misfortune and happiness alike. We are never as bad off or as happy as we say we are. (Honoré de Balzac)

Balzac: Wisdom is that apprehension of heavenly things to which the spirit rises through love. (Honoré de Balzac)

Churchill: Courage is rightly esteemed the first of human qualities... because it is the quality which guarantees all others.

Churchill: I never worry about action, but only inaction.

Dediu: Common sense is essential for success, and education helps.

Dediu: New skills encourage success.

Dediu: One way to achieve success is to do what you like, you know well and it is useful for many people.

Dediu: To be successful, you need to sell.

Dediu - Triumph causes self-righteousness.
Self-righteousness causes laziness.
Laziness. causes fiasco.

Edison: Being busy does not always mean real work.

Edison: Seeming to do is not doing.

Edison: The object of all work is production or accomplishment and to either of these ends there must be forethought, system, planning, intelligence, and honest purpose, as well as perspiration.

Edison: The value of an idea lies in the using of it.

Edison: There is far more opportunity than there is ability.

Edison: There is no expedient to which a man will not go to avoid the labor of thinking.
Edison: There is no substitute for hard work.

Edison: There's a way to do it better - find it.

Edison: To have a great idea, have a lot of them.

Edison: To invent, you need a good imagination and a pile of junk.

Edison: Waste is worse than loss. The time is coming when every person who lays claim to ability will keep the question of waste before him constantly. The scope of thrift is limitless.

Edison: What a man's mind can create, man's character can control.

Edison: What you are, will show in what you do.

Edison: When I have fully decided that a result is worth getting, I go ahead of it and make trial after trial until it comes.

Edison: Your worth consists in what you are and not in what you have.

Edison: Discontent is the first necessity of progress.

Edison: Everything comes to him who hustles while he waits.

Edison: I find my greatest pleasure, and so my reward, in the work that precedes what the world calls success.

Edison: I have not failed. I've just found 10,000 ways that won't work.

Edison: I never did a day's work in my life. It was all fun.

Edison: I start where the last man left off.

Edison: If we did all the things we are capable of, we would literally astound ourselves.

Edison: It is astonishing what an effort it seems to be for many people to put their brains definitely and systematically to work.

Edison: Just because something doesn't do what you planned it to do, doesn't mean it's useless.

Edison: Nearly every man who develops an idea works it up to the point where it looks impossible, and then he gets discouraged. That's not the place to become discouraged.

Edison: Opportunity is missed by most people because it is dressed in overalls and looks like work.

Edison: The best thinking has been done in solitude. The worst has been done in turmoil.

Edison: The three great essentials to achieve anything worthwhile are: Hard work, Stick-to-itiveness, and Common sense.

Epicurus: It is folly for a man to pray to the gods for that which he has the power to obtain by himself.

Epicurus: Skillful pilots gain their reputation from storms and tempest.

Fierce and mighty - Acerbus et ingens
Example: "For success one needs to be acerbus et ingens."

Follow the money - Sequere pecuniam

For the glory - Ad gloriam
Example: "Many artists work hard ad gloriam."

He conquers who conquers himself - Vincit qui se vincit
Example: "First you need self-discipline and self-control, because vincit qui se vincit."

Horace: Begin, be bold and venture to be wise.
Horace: Choose a subject equal to your abilities; think carefully what your shoulders may refuse, and what they are capable of bearing.

Horace: He who feared he would not succeed sat still - Sedit qui timuit ne non succederet

Example: "Move ahead, because only sedit qui timuit ne non succederet."

Horace: If you can better these principles, tell me; if not, join me in following them Si quid novisti rectius istis, candidus imperti; si nil, his utere mecum

Example: "Refering to the ideas from this book: si quid novisti rectius istis, candidus imperti; si nil, his utere mecum."

Horace: He has the deed half-done, who has made a beginning.

If the end is good, everything will be good) - Si finis bonus est, totum bonum erit

Example: "After all the ups and downs, si finis bonus est, totum bonum erit."

I'll either find a way or make one - Aut viam inveniam aut faciam

Example: "Great commanders and achievers many times say aut viam inveniam aut faciam."

I repel adversity by valor - Adversa virtute repello
Example: "Unfortunately, there is much adversity in the world, but everybody should say adversa virtute repello".

I seek higher things - Altiora peto

Example: "If success is the objective, then you should always say altiora peto."

Mode of operation - Modus operandi

Example: "Anybody who works for achieving a certain result needs a modus operandi."

Napoleon: Nothing is more difficult, and therefore more precious, than to be able to decide.

Ovid: Be patient and tough; someday this pain will be useful to you - Perfer et obdura; dolor hic tibi proderit olim

Example: "To be successful you'll have to pass through some painful situations, but perfer et obdura; dolor hic tibi proderit olim."

Ovid: A horse never runs so fast as when he has other horses to catch up and outpace.

Ovid: A new idea is delicate. It can be killed by a sneer or a yawn; it can be stabbed to death by a quip and worried to death by a frown on the right man's brow.

Ovid: Either do not attempt at all, or go through with it.

Ovid: The will is commendable, though the ability may be wanting.

Ovid: Courage conquers all things: it even gives strength to the body.

Ovid: I attempt an arduous task; but there is no worth in that which is not a difficult achievement.

Ovid: It is the poor man who'll ever count his flock.

Ovid: The burden which is well borne becomes light.

Ovid: The prayers of cowards fortune spurns.

Ovid: The spirited horse, which will try to win the race of its own accord, will run even faster if encouraged.

Ovid: Venus favors the bold.

Plato: A hero is born among a hundred, a wise man is found among a thousand, but an accomplished one might not be found even among a hundred thousand men.

Plato: All things will be produced in superior quantity and quality, and with greater ease, when each man works at a single occupation, in accordance with his natural gifts, and at the right moment, without meddling with anything else.

Plato: Apply yourself both now and in the next life. Without effort, you cannot be prosperous. Though the land be good, you cannot have an abundant crop without cultivation.

Plato: The builders say, the larger stones do not lie well without the lesser.

Plato: Better a little which is well done, than a great deal imperfectly.

Plato: For a man to conquer himself is the first and noblest of all victories.

Plato: I never did anything worth doing by accident, nor did any of my inventions come by accident; they came by work.

Plato: Necessity... the mother of invention.

Plato: The beginning is the most important part of the work.

Plato: The man who makes everything that leads to happiness depends upon himself, and not upon other men, has adopted the very best plan for living happily.

This is the man of moderation, the man of manly character and of wisdom.

Second to none - Nulli secundus
    Example: "Our team is nulli secundus."

Seneca: If you want to be loved, love - Si vis amari, ama

Seneca: There is no easy way from the earth to the stars - Non est ad astra mollis e terris via
    Example: "Sooner or later everybody find out that non est ad astra mollis e terris via."

Virgil: They can because they think they can - Possunt quia posse videntur
    Example: "Looking at big achievers, Virgil's words come to mind: Possunt quia posse videntur."

We all have power to do harm - Ad nocendum patentes sumus
    Example: "Even if ad nocendum patentes sumus, we should always try not to do harm."

Through difficulties to the stars! - Per aspera ad astra!
     Example: "How do we achieve great results? Per aspera ad astra!"
Here we have a nice poem too.

Per Aspera Ad Astra
(Through Difficulties To The Stars)
by
Michael M. Dediu

Per aspera ad astra
Said the Romans long ago.
Let a Universe orchestra,
Start a grand and cosmic show.

Study physics, mathematics,
Perdurable chemistry;
Then with bioastronautics,
See what's new in geometry.

Now nanotechnology
Is the future for the space.
Fly ad astra, use pomology,
To see, friend, moon's other face.

Sic itur ad astra means
Such's the way to stars.
Work to reach antipodeans
At the Universe altars.

Every breath you take,
Make it an abutment.
For the move you make,
To be an achievement.

Make the Universe gallant...

Learn much more than yesterday.
Dare be happy and more volant.
Make some progress every day!

To the stars through difficulties - Ad astra per aspera
   Example: "Is it easy to be successful? Well, ad astra per aspera."

To work is to pray - Laborare est orare
   Example: "For many great achievers, laborare est orare."

Who dares wins - Qui audet adipiscitur
Example: "You need to dare, because only qui audet adipiscitur."

Yield not to misfortunes, but advance ever more boldly against them - Tu ne cede malis sed contra audentior ito
   Example: "Bad things happen, however tu ne cede malis sed contra audentior ito."

Chapter I. 3 – Time

At another day - Ad alium diem
    Example: "The mathematical analysis of this subject was deferred ad alium diem."

At the age of – Aetatis
    Example: "He began to study advanced mathematics aetatis 17."

At the beginning - Ad initium

Augustus Caesar: The play is over, applaud! Acta est fabula, plaudite!
    Example: "The last words of the Roman Emperor Augustus Caesar were: acta est fabula, plaudite!"

Byron: In her first passion, a woman loves her lover, in all the others all she loves is love. (Lord Byron - British Poet)

Dediu: Time is so precious and so little, you never know when it's gone.

Do not redo that which has been done - Actum ne agas
    Example: "In this software development task, please actum ne agas."

Epicurus: The time when most of you should withdraw into yourself is when you are forced to be in a crowd.

Forever and ever - Seculo seculorum

Farewell forever - Aeternum vale
    Example: "After many successful years of teaching, the professor decided to say aeternum vale."

For a few days - Ad paucos dies
    Example: "After they were in vacation ad paucos dies in Rome, they returned very happy and ready for work."

For eternal life; for all time - Ad vitam aeternam
    Example: "This classical symphonic music is ad vitam aeternam."

For life; for the duration of a person's life - Ad vitam
    Example: "Some honorific positions are given ad vitam."

For life or until a misdeed - Ad vitam aut culpam
    Example: "There are judges who are appointed ad vitam aut culpam."

From that day - A die
> *Example*: "One day last year they had a great victory; a die they did not succeed anymore."

From the beginning - Ab initio
> *Example*: "We have to start this analysis ab initio."

From the cradle - Ab incunabulis
> *Example*: "This child appeared to be smart ab incunabulis."

From the date - A dato
> *Example*: "We'll start the inspection a dato when the building is finished."

From the egg - Ab ovo
Another translation can be "from the beginning".
The point in time or space at which anything begins. The act or process of bringing or being brought into being; a start. In the Ars Poetica (The Art of Poetry or On the Nature of Poetry), the Latin poet Horace praises Homer that in his Iliad he stated that the Troy war started from the Greek Achilles hero's anger and not **ab ovo**, that is not from the birth of Helen, who according to the legend was born from the Leda's egg. (Troy was a city, both factual and legendary, located in northwest Anatolia in what is now Turkey, southeast of the Dardanelles and beside Mount Ida. The place is best known for being the place of the Trojan War described in the Greek Epic Cycle and especially in the Iliad, one of the two epic poems attributed to Homer)
> *Example*: "There is no sufficient time now to start ab ovo.

From eternity - Ab aeterno
> *Example*: "Our universe is ab aeterno."

From the foundation of the city (i.e., Rome) - Ab urbe condita
 Example: "This tradition here in Rome is ab urbe condita."

From the origin - Ab origine
 Example: "To better understand this situation, we have to start ab origine."

Horace: From the egg to the apples - Ab ovo usque ad mala
 Example: "When we want to describe something from the beginning to the end we'll say: let's discuss this subject ab ovo usque ad mala."

Horace: Clogged with yesterday's excess, the body drags the mind down with it.

Horace: Cease to inquire what the future has in store, and take as a gift whatever the day brings forth.

In the time between; in the meantime; for the time being; temporary - Ad interim
    Example: "The management appointed an ad interim team of engineers to inspect the production problems."

In the year of his age – Anno aetatis suae
    Example: "The great ancient Roman poet Publius Vergilius Maro (Virgil) died anno 19 BC aetatis suae 49."

It lacks a beginning and an end - Caret initio et fine
    Example: "His presentation is good, but caret initio et fine."

More durable than bronze; everlasting - Aere perennius
    Example: "There are many aere perennius monuments in Rome."

Ovid: Neither can the wave that has passed by be recalled, nor the hour which has passed return again.

Ovid: Everything comes gradually and at its appointed hour.

Ovid: Time is the devourer of all things.

Ovid: Time, motion and wine cause sleep.

Ovid: At times it is folly to hasten, at other times, to delay. The wise do everything in its proper time.

Ovid: Use the occasion, for it passes swiftly

Plato: It is a common saying, and in everybody's mouth, that life is but a sojourn.

Plato: To suffer the penalty of too much haste, which is too little speed.
Pythagoras: Reason is immortal, all else mortal.

Rousseau: Most nations, as well as people, are impossible only in their youth; they become incorrigible as they grow older. (Jean-Jacques Rousseau - Philosopher)

The City (Rome) Foundation Year - Anno Urbis Contitae (AUC)
    Example: "For Rome, by tradition, Anno Urbis Contitae (AUC) is set in 753 BC."

Time flies - Tempus fugit
    Example: "With the age, one begins to notice that tempus fugit faster and faster..."

To do what has already been done - Actum agree
    Example: "In this project there is a lot of repetition, waste of time, unnecessary work and labor in vain, because they have actum agere."

To infinity; without end; without limit - Ad infinitum
    Example: "There is no activity which can go ad infinitum."

To many years - Ad multos annos
    Example: "At his birthday everybody wished him ad multos annos!"

To the end; at the end of the page - Ad finem
    Example: "Those people supported their team ad finem."

To the extreme (i.e., to the end) - Ad extremum

Example: "They want to continue their exploration of this territory ad extremum."

Virgil: From Jove is the beginning - Ab Iove principium
It can be translated also: Let's start with Jupiter.
It is from Virgil, Eclogue III. The Eclogues is the first of the three major works, pastorals, of the Latin poet Virgil. He takes as his generic model the Greek Bucolica ("On care of cattle", poem in which shepherds converse). Literally it means to start from the most important person (because Jupiter was considered the chief of the Gods), or from the most important thing.
This expression is used at the beginning of a debate or an exposure, signaling that we'll start with the most important, or the principal assertion.
Example: "We'll have our presentation ab Iove principium."

Chapter I. 4 - Education

A blank tablet (about a student's mind) - Tabula rasa
    Example: "Before receiving the impressions gained from experience, the human mind, especially at birth, is tabula rasa."

A great work - Magnum opus
    Example: "Usually the greatest masterpiece of a writer or a composer is called magnum opus."

Acts of the scholars - Acta Eruditorum
    Example: "For 100 years, between 1682 and 1782, Acta Eruditorum was the first scientific journal of the German lands, initially published in Leipzig."

Aeschylus: I'm not afraid of storms, for I'm learning to sail my ship.

Against good morals - Adversus bonos mores
    Example: "Unfortunately, there are too many things these days, which are adversus bonos mores."

At the Greek calends (i.e., never, as Greeks did not have calends) - Ad calendas Graecas
    Example: "It looks like this work will be finished ad calendas Graecas."

At the opening of a book - Ad aperturam libri
    Example: "It is nice to be careful and concentrated ad aperturam libri."

Aristotle: The roots of education are bitter, but the fruit is sweet.

Aristotle: It is the mark of an educated mind to be able to entertain a thought without accepting it.

Balzac: A mother who is really a mother is never free. (Honoré de Balzac)

Balzac: Study lends a kind of enchantment to all our surroundings.

Boethius: If you had kept your silence, you would have stayed a philosopher - Si tacuisses, philosophus mansisses

Churchill: Broadly speaking, the short words are the best, and the old words best of all.

Cicero: Constant practice devoted to one subject often outdoes both intelligence and skill- Assiduus usus uni rei deditus et ingenium et artem saepe vincit

      Example: "Many people who concentrated on a sigle subject, sooner or later noticed that assiduus usus uni rei deditus et ingenium et artem saepe vincit."

Cicero: One should employ restraint in his jests - Adhibenda est in iocando moderatio
Example: "Listening to some of the unrestrained, immoral and uncivilized jests of these days, we all ask that everybody should respect Cicero's rule: adhibenda est in iocando moderatio."

Dediu: Be more hungry for knowledge than for food.

Dediu: Even a drop of education can change the color of an ocean of ignorance.

Dediu: Computers are tools for education, not substitutes of it.

Dediu: If we are over 30, we should ask not what our parents can do for us, but what we can do for our parents.

Diligence is a very great help, even to a mediocre intelligence - Diligentia maximum etiam mediocris ingeni subsidium
Example: "It is important for parents and teachers to cultivate industry and perseverance in children, because diligentia maximum etiam mediocris ingeni subsidium."

Edison: We don't know a millionth of one percent about anything.

Either learn or leave - Aut disce aut discede
Example: "At that advanced school of mathematics, you aut disce aut discede."

Experience teaches - Experientia docet
Example: "Even if you have many years of good schooling, still experientia docet much more."

For the Dauphin's use; expurgated - Ad usum Delphini
　　Example: "When some texts are purified, to be used by young people, one can say these texts are ad usum Delphini."

Good listener, hello! - À bon entendeur, salut! (French.)
The significance of this expression is: who has ears to hear, hear or listen up. Intentionally, the expression is used in original, to entice the audience's attention, with the understanding that there is much more to the matter which cannot be said completely.
　　Example: "For now, I said enough! À bon entendeur, salut!"

He who writes reads twice - Qui scribit bis legit
　　Example: "One who wants to remember something that he was reading, it is recommended to write it, because qui scribit bis legit."

Horace - A man accomplished to his fingertips - Ad unguem factus homo
　　Example: "That man has achieved very much in all directions, he is ad unguem factus homo."

Horace: A word once uttered can never be recalled.

It is difficult to retain what you may have learned unless you practice it - Difficile est tenere quae acceperis nisi exerceas
　　Example: "As the years pass by, we all notice that difficile est tenere quae acceperis nisi exerceas."

Kind mother (old students about their university) - Alma mater
　　Example: "Many graduates from known universities remember with nostalgia their alma mater."

Know thyself - Nosce te ipsum

Knowledge itself is power - Ipsa scientia potestas est
    Example: "If one does not know much, it is difficult to get power, because ipsa scientia potestas est."
Here we have to repeat our maxim:
    Few people know,
    How much you have to know,
    To know,
    How little you know.

Not for me, not for you, but for us - Non mihi, non tibi, sed nobis
    Example: "When an award is given to our team, then we can say that this award is non mihi, non tibi, sed nobis."

Ovid: You can learn from anyone, even your enemy.

Plato: And what, Socrates, is the food of the soul? Surely, I said, knowledge is the food of the soul.

Plato: For good nurture and education implant good constitutions.

Plato: If a man neglects education, he walks lame to the end of his life.

Plato: Ignorance, the root and stem of all evil.

Plato: Knowledge is true opinion.

Plato: Knowledge which is acquired under compulsion obtains no hold on the mind.

Plato: Let parents bequeath to their children not riches, but the spirit of reverence.

Plato: Music is the movement of sound to reach the soul for the education of its virtue.

Plato: No man should bring children into the world, who is unwilling to persevere to the end in their nature and education.

Plato: Opinion is the medium between knowledge and ignorance.

Plato: The direction in which education starts a man will determine his future in life.

Plato: The learning and knowledge that we have, is, at the most, but little compared with that of which we are ignorant.

Plato: There is no harm in repeating a good thing.

Plato: Twice and thrice over, as they say, good is it to repeat and review what is good.

Plato: We ought to esteem it of the greatest importance, that the fictions, which children first hear, should be adapted in the most perfect manner to the promotion of virtue.

Repetition is the mother of studies - Repetitio est mater studiorum
   Example: "From the very young age everybody learns that repetitio est mater studiorum.*"*

Rousseau: However great a man's natural talent may be, the act of writing cannot be learned all at once. (Jean-Jacques Rousseau - Philosopher)

Seneca: Men learn while they teach - Homines dum docent discunt
   Example: "Teaching is a great way of learning, because homines dum docent discunt."

Seneca: Ignorance is the cause of fear - Timendi causa est nescire
   Example: "The more we know, the better we understand, because timendi causa est nescire."

Silence is golden - Silentium est aureum

Slip of memory - Lapsus memoriae

Slip of the hand - Lapsus manus

Slip of the pen - Lapsus calami

Slip of the tongue - Lapsus linguae

So let us rejoice - Gaudeamus igitur
   Example: "For more than 200 years, the oldest student song is Gaudeamus igitur."

Something to be added - Addendum
Example: "Many scientific and technical books need to add some explanations, and each of them uses an addendum."

Teach in order to learn (we learn by teaching) - Docendo discimus

    Example: "If you really want to learn well a certain difficult subject, then docendo discimus."

To honor through difficulties - Ad augusta per angusta

    Example: "The road to high places many times passes through narrow and difficult paths, and the same we can say ad augusta per angusta."

To the word; verbatim - Ad verbum

    Example: "Please translate this letter ad verbum."

Virgil: It is imperative to be well trained in the early youth - Adeo in teneris consuescere multum est

    Example: "Any parent and grandparent should know that adeo in teneris consuescere multum est."

Chapter I. 5 - Practical

According to custom, to usage - Ad usum
    Example: "If a company has a subsidiary in another country, that subsidiary has to operate ad usum for that country."

According to; like - Ad instar
    Example: "The engineer was appointed as manager, ad instar the rules of the company."

According to value - Ad valorem
    Example: "Taxes on property are assessed ad valorem of that property."

After death - Post mortem
    Example: "There are many writers and composers who became famous only post mortem."

Against; contrary to – Adversus
    Example: "He had a point of view adversus the opinion of his colleague."

All to one; in a unanimous fashion - Ad unum omnes
    Example: "After many discussions, the decision was adopted ad unum omnes."

And also - Ac etiam
    Example: "We had to solve many cases ac etiam to help some other teams."

Another of the same kind; second self - Alter idem
    Example: "For their project they had a powerful computer, but they needed alter idem."

Another way must be tried - Alia tentanda via est
    Example: "When a certain method for solving a problem is not successful, alia tentanda via est."

Appeal to respect or modesty in an argument - Ad verecundiam
    Example: "In his presentation, the consultant made an ad verecundiam in order to justify his request."

Appius Claudius Caecus: Every man is the maker of his own fortune - Faber est suae quisque fortunae
    Example: "The professor emphasized the importance of self-responsibility, because faber est suae quisque fortunae."

At hand (i.e., ready and prepared) - Ad manum
    Example: "This consultant is ad manum to provide necessary services."

At my own risk - Meo periculo
    Example: "I decided, meo periculo, to start a project, which everybody was saying that cannot be done."

At one's pleasure - A bene placito
    Example: "After a great effort to finish the software project, the engineer had some free time a bene placito."

At pleasure; extemporaneously or freely - Ad libitum (ad lib)

Example: "This musical piece has an ad libitum part, for improvisations.

At the place, at a specific location - Ad locum
Example: "We plan this building to be ad locum."

At this place - Ad hunc locum

Balzac: A woman knows the face of the man she loves as a sailor knows the open sea. (Honoré de Balzac)
Example: "Our new house will be built ad hunc locum."

Bath - Balneum
Example: "The very popular balneum had been appreciated by Romans starting before 250 BC."

By the fact itself - Ipso facto
Example: "Doing a bad product, the worker was condemned ipso facto."

Caesar: From the bottom of the heart - Ab imo pectore
Example: "Julius Caesar used to address to his people with sincerity and ab imo pectore."

Candor gives wings to strength - Candor dat viribus alas
Example: "After many years of experience, he noticed that candor dat viribus alas."

Divide and rule or **Divide and conquer** or **Divide in order to conquer** - Divide et impera
Example: "In the fight against the growth of the health care costs, a good idea is to use the Roman method divide et impera."

Do not disturb - Noli perturbare

Example: "A beautiful classical music could be heard from a music class, and on the door was a sign: Noli perturbare."

Do not enter; keep out - Noli intrare
Example: "There was a special laboratory in the company, with a clear sign on the door: noli intrare."

Do what you are doing (i.e., pay attention to what you are doing) - Age quod agis
Example: "In order to have a work of good quality, it is important to age quod agis."

Each needs the help of the other - Alterum alterius auxilio eget
Example: "To solve a complicated technical emergency, alterum alterius auxilio eget."

Envy absent (i.e., no offense intended) - Absit invidia
Example: "The manager critized an engineer, but absit invidia."

Equably and diligently - Aequabiliter et diligenter
Example: "The conference was managed aequabiliter et diligenter."

Every other day - Alternis diebus
Example: "The engineer had access to some sophisticated equipment alternis diebus."

Every other hour - Alternis horis
Example: "For a short period of time, the child had to take some medications alternis horis."

Faithful to the end - Ad finem fidelis

Example: "The supporters of this team were ad finem fidelis."

First among equals - Primus inter pares
Example: "There were several good engineers in this company, but Michael was primus inter pares."

For reference; for further consideration - Ad referendum
Example: "This agreement is ad referendum, and needs to be approved by a manager."

For this; for a specific occasion; impromptu - Ad hoc
Example: "To improve the quality, a manager was selected ad hoc."

From another point of view - Alio intuit
Example: "After the consultant gave an explanation of the project, the manager approached the project alio intuitu."

From head to heel (totally, entirely) - A capite ad calcem
Example: "This lady is in red a capite ad calcem."

From the angry man (i.e., unfair) - Ab irato
Example: "This manager took some ab irato decisions, which are not good for his team."

From the older ox the younger learns to plow - Ab ove maiori discit arare minor

Example: "The older generation has to teach the younger one many practical things, because ab ove maiori discit arare minor."

From the outside - Ab extra
 Example: "That team has received significant help ab extra."

From the past one can infer the future - Ab actu ad posse valet illation
 Example: "What has happened is always important, because ab actu ad posse valet illation."

From the side; with confidence - A latere
 Example: "This project has a task a latere, but it is important."

From within - Ab intra
 Example: "The energy and the desire for success must come ab intra."

Go in peace (one of the Roman "goodbye" expressions) - Vade in pace
 Example: "After a good meeting, we said to each other vade in pace."

He who quarrel with a drunk, hurts an absentee - Absentem laedit cum ebrio qui litigat
 Example: "It is much better to help a drunk to go to an assistance center, and not to quarrel with him, because absentem laedit cum ebrio qui litigat."

Horace: He who has begun is half done - Dimidium facti, qui coepit habet
 Example: "It is important to start well a project, because dimidium facti, qui coepit habet."

Horace: Avoid inquisitive persons, for they are sure to be gossips, their ears are open to hear, but they will not keep what is entrusted to them.

I am present; to be present – Adsum
      Example: "An important decision is discussed at this meeting and adsum."
In short; in a word - Ad summam

In the likeness of all - Ad instar omnium
      Example: "The portret of the team was ad instar omnium."

In the manner of; consistent with - Ad modum
      Example: "This young poet tries to write ad modum Horace."

Irresistible urge to do something inadvisable – Cacoethes
      Example: "This worker has a cacoethes for smoking."

Let it be increased – Additur
      Example: "This team decided to spend for the new computer the amount of $500, but the manager said additur by $200."

Let us turn to better things - Ad meliora vertamur
      Example: "An old man observed a group of young people wasting their time with inutile controversies, and kindly told them ad meliora vertamur."

May he love tomorrow who has never loved before; and may he who has loved, love tomorrow as well - Cras amet qui nunquam amavit; quique amavit, cras amet

Example: "A beautiful homage to the importance of love is this: cras amet qui nunquam amavit; quique amavit, cras amet."

May the omen be absent (i.e., God forbid) - Absit omen
Example: "If this computer does not work, absit omen, we will be in big trouble."

Means of support (i.e., food, clothing, shelter) – Alimenta
Example: "A welfare program for orphans first needs alimenta."

Mountain air - Afflatus montium
Example: "When they visited Utah and Switzerland, they could feel the pleasant afflatus montium."

Napoleon: The best way to keep one's word is not to give it.

Never despair - Nil desperandum
Example: "When the students are with their professor of mathematics, they nil desperandum."

No way - Nullo modo

Example: "Maybe we can postpone this work, somebody said; nullo modo, responded the manager."

Note well - Nota bene
Example: "I explain here some details of our work, and, nota bene, there are special security issues."

On alternate nights - Alternis noctibus
Example: "For security reason, the passwords had to be changed alternis noctibus."

On the first view - Prima facie
Example: "This software project, prima facie, seemed easy, but shortly it was noticed that there are many difficulties."

One's second self; other I - Alter ego
Example: "Sometimes I have debates with myself on an issue, and it looks like a debate between me and my alter ego."

Ovid: Add a little to a little and there will be a great pile - Adde parvum parvo magnus acervus erit
Example: "We all notice from experience that if you adde parvum parvo magnus acervus erit."

Ovid: Studies change into habits - Abeunt studia in mores
Example: "Very good education is so important, because abeunt studia in mores."

Ovid: Luck affects everything. Let your hook always be cast; in the stream where you least expect, it there will be a fish.

Ovid: If you want to be loved, be lovable.

Plato: To love rightly is to love what is orderly and beautiful in an educated and disciplined way.

Publius Syrus: He conquers twice who conquers himself in victory - Bis vincit qui se vincit in victoria
    Example: "In sport, the victorious team was kind with the defeated one, because bis vincit qui se vincit in victoria."
Rousseau: Insults are the arguments employed by those who are in the wrong. (Jean-Jacques Rousseau - Philosopher)

Shake or stir – Agita
    Example: "It is recommended to agita many juices before you drink them."

That is - Id est
    Example: "The engineer explained this project in detail, id est he gave all the tasks which need to be performed."

The same – Idem
    Example: "The presenter gave the name of a book at beginning, then later, referring to this book, said: compare idem."

The state in which things are now; the existing state of affairs - Status quo
    Example: "In many countries the governments want to preserve the status quo, but the people want changes for better living conditions."

The other way around; the terms being reversed - Vice versa
    Example: "When law becomes bad, morals are bad, and vice versa."

To be administered – Adhibendus
> *Example:* "The doctor recommended a certain medicine adhibendus."

To be present – Adesse
> *Example:* "When the conference will begin they want adesse."

To one's taste - Ad gustum
> *Example:* "When the group went to a restaurant, everyone ordered ad gustum."

To pity (i.e., appealing to mercy) - Ad misericordiam
> *Example:* "Not being able to get an approval for his project, the contractor tried ad misericordiam arguments."

To saturation - Ad saturatum
> *Example:* "They discussed this subject ad saturatum."

To the damages (i.e., amount demanded) - Ad damnum
> *Example:* "There were some damages to the car and ad damnum was $1000."

To the fingernail (i.e., with great precision) - Ad unguem
> *Example:* "The expert tested the smoothness of a telescopic mirror and said with satisfaction: it is ad unguem."

To the highest point – Adsummum
> *Example:* "Working with dedication on many projects, this team arrived adsummum."

To the letter (i.e., precisely) - Ad litteram

Example: "Many translations are required to be ad litteram."

To the people - Ad populum
Example: "All politicians address ad populum, and say what the people want to hear."

To the person; relating to the individual - Ad personal
Example: "This company produces ad personal items."

To the point of sickness; to nausea; to the point of being disgusted - Ad nauseam
Example: "Sometime politicians repeat a certain topic ad nauseam."

To the point; relevant to the present matter - Ad rem
Example: "We have an important issue here, and let's have the discussions ad rem."

To the same point - Ad idem
Example: "The two engineers finally arrived ad idem regarding the solution for a technical problem."

To what damage - Ad quod damnum
Example: "When there is an accident, there are discussions about the amount to be paid ad quod damnum."

Virgil: Carry on and preserve yourselves for better times - Durate et vosmet rebus servate secundis

Example: "The team was working hard on a difficult project, and the manager told them durate et vosmet rebus servate secundis."

Virgil: *From one example, learn all* - Ab uno disce omnes
Example: "There are cases where just from a single example, all can learn a general truth, therefore ab uno disce omnes."

Virgil: *Love conquers all* - Amor vincit Omnia
Example: "It is an eternal truth that amor vincit omnia."

Virgil: *Ready for both; prepared for either alternative* - Ad utrumque paratus
Example: "A good emergency team is ad utrumque paratus."

With even stronger reason; all the more - A fortiori
Example: "This project was completed, therefore, a fortiori, a particular task from the project was also completed.

With God's help, work prospers - Adiuvante Deo labor proficit
Example: "An old man was looking at the efforts after an earthquake and said adiuvante Deo labor proficit."

Without a day; indefinitely - Sine die
Explanation: It is originally from the old common law texts, where it indicates that a final, dispositive order has been made in a case. In modern legal context, it means there is nothing left for the court to do, so no date for further proceedings is set.
Example: "Our meeting was postponed sine die."

Without which it could not be; essential - Sine qua non
    Example: "A sine qua non condition for happiness is morality."

What's new? - Quid novi?
    Example: "When the manager came back, he asked: quid novi?"

Whether you like it or not - Volens nolens
    Explanation: It is also used in the form **Nolens volens** – Unwilling, willing. That is, "whether unwillingly or willingly". Sometimes expressed **aut nolens aut volens** or **nolentis volentis**. It is similar to willy-nilly, though that word is derived from Old English will-he nil-he ([whether] he will or [whether] he will not).
    Example: "You received this task, and, volens nolens, you have to do it."

While I breathe, I hope - Dum spiro, spero
    Example: "In the middle of great difficulties, I always remember that dum spiro, spero."

While there is life, there is hope - Dum vita est spes est
    Example: "Sometimes it appears that there is no hope, but dum vita est spes est."

Wonderful to tell - Mirabile dictum
    Example: "We were visiting Rome, and, mirabile dictum, the Trajan's column, erected in 113 AD, appears before us."

Wonderful to see - Mirabile visu
    Example: "It is always mirabile visu the progress of these children at school."

Chapter I. 6 - Law

Abuse does not remove use - Abusus non tollit usum
Example: "If someone drink too much beer, it does not mean to make beer illegal, because abusus non tollit usum."

Act of God - Actus Dei
Example: "When there is actus Dei, all people help."

Against common law - Contra ius commune
Example: "This worker did something which was contra ius commune."

Against the law of nations - Contra ius gentium
Example: "In international business it is important not to act contra ius gentium."

Balzac: Laws are spider webs through which the big flies pass and the little ones get caught. (Honoré de Balzac)

Cicero: We are slaves of the law so that that we may be free - Legum servi sumus ut liberi esse possimus
Example: "If only one is free and the others are not – this is dictatorship. We can have freedom for everybody, if we all comply with the law, therefore: legum servi sumus ut liberi esse possimus."

Concerning the law; legally - De jure (de iure)
Example: "This company has fulfilled its legal requirements, therefore it is a De Jure Company."

Consent makes the law - Consensus facit legem

Example: "If there is consent about a contract between two parties, then the contract becomes law, because consensus facit legem."

Elsewhere - Alibi
Example: "He used an alibi excuse, not to be blamed for an accident."

Equity follows the law - Aequitas sequitur legem
Example: "Impartiality is essential in applying the law, and for this we have aequitas sequitur legem."

Gross fault - Culpa lata
Example: "This person has committed a culpa lata and he will be punished."

Horace: Punishment follows closely behind crime's heels - Culpam poena premit comes
Example: "It is good for everybody to know that culpam poena premit comes."

Horace: Fidelity is the sister of justice.

I absolve; I acquit – Absolvo
Example: "After a short deliberation about a minor error of a student, the professor said absolvo."

Let the punishment fit the crime - Culpae poenae par esto
Example: "This is what all the good people are saying for thousands of years: culpae poenae par esto."

Lucilius: They consent to laws, which place people outside the law - Accipiunt leges, populus quibus legibus ex lex
Example: "A sign of dictatorship is when accipiunt leges, populus quibus legibus ex lex."

Money belonging to another; a debt - Aes alienum
Example: "The company discovered that an important amount of money was actually aes alienum."

My fault - Mea culpa
Example: "Example: "When you make a mistake, simply say mea culpa."

No man shall be a judge in his own cause - Nemo iudex in causa sua
Explanation: Legal principle that no individual can preside over a hearing in which he holds a specific interest or bias.
Example: "If you are in dispute with another person, you cannot be a judge in this dispute, because nemo iudex in causa sua."

Ordinary negligence - Culpa levis
Example: "Being a culpa levis for this young man, he will be sent for more training and education."

Ovid: Alas! How difficult it is not to betray one's guilt by one's looks.

Ovid: The penalty may be removed, the crime is eternal.

Ovid: What is deservedly suffered must be borne with calmness, but when the pain is unmerited, the grief is resistless.

Plato: Good people do not need laws to tell them to act responsibly, while bad people will find a way around the laws.

Plato: Injustice is censured because the censures are afraid of suffering, and not from any fear which they have of doing injustice.

Plato: Justice in the life and conduct of the State is possible only as first it resides in the hearts and souls of the citizens.

Plato: Justice means minding one's own business and not meddling with other men's concerns.

Plato: Man never legislates, but destinies and accidents, happening in all sorts of ways, legislate in all sorts of ways.

Plato: No law or ordinance is mightier than understanding.

Plato: Not to help justice in its need would be an impiety.

Plato: The highest reach of injustice is to be deemed just when you are not.

Plato: To go to the world below, having a soul which is like a vessel full of injustice, is the last and worst of all the evils.

Plato: When a Benefit is wrongly conferred, the author of the Benefit may often be said to injure.

Pythagoras: As soon as laws are necessary for men, they are no longer fit for freedom.

Tacitus: In a very corrupt state are the most laws - Corruptissima re publica plurimae leges

    Example: "When there is much corruption, then more laws are needed to try to eliminate different types of corruption, therefore corruptissima re publica plurimae leges."

The absent one will not be beneficiary - Absense haeres non erit

    Example: "Mark was not present at the discussions; therefore we'll apply the rule absens haeres non erit."

The law does not concern itself with trifles - De minimis non curat lex

    Example: "When somebody does a minor legal mistake, no court intervention is necessary, because de minimis non curat lex."

The law does not distinguish and so we ought not distinguish - Lex non distinguitur nos non distinguere debemus

    Example: "There are places where the law is not the same for all, and we have to reiterate that lex non distinguitur nos non distinguere debemus."

The law is harsh, but it is the law - Dura lex sed lex

Example: "Some may not like a severe punishment, but dura lex sed lex."

This is harsh but the law is written - Durum hoc est sed ita lex scripta est
Example: "Sometimes the punishment appears to be hard, but they say durum hoc est sed ita lex scripta est."

To judgment; to common sense - Ad iudicium
Example: "When making a decision, let's not forget to be ad iudicium."

Without any marks - Absque ulla nota
Example: "After a team analyzed a good proposal, they approved it absque ulla nota."

You may approach the court - Accedas ad curiam
Example: "When you are ready, accedas ad curiam."

Chapter I. 7 - Miscellanea

A precipice in front and wolves behind (between a rock and a hard place) - A fronte praecipitium a tergo lupi
   Example: "When you find yourself in a situation like with a fronte praecipitium a tergo lupi, do not despair and ask for help."

Abracadabra
This term originated from cabalists (a mystical sect from Middle Ages Jewish people). A kind of occult theosophy or traditional interpretation of the Scriptures among Jewish rabbis and certain medieval Christians, which treats of the nature of god and the mystery of human existence. It assumes that every letter, word, number, and accent of Scripture contains a hidden sense; and it teaches the methods of interpretation for ascertaining these occult meanings. The cabalists pretend even to foretell events by this means.   It is formed from the abbreviation of the Hebraic words Ab (father), Ben (son), Abraham or bat Abraham (son or daughter of Abraham)
Abracadabra was used as magical formula against various pains. It is used by magicians as an introductory formula in their prestidigitation work . (Performance of or skill in performing magic or conjuring tricks with the hands)
   Judaism (from the Latin Iudaismus, derived from the Greek Ioudaïsmos, and ultimately from the Hebrew יהודה, Yehudah, "Judah"; in Hebrew: יַהֲדוּת . Yahedut, the distinctive characteristics of the Judean *ethnos*) is the religion, philosophy, and way of life of the Jewish people. Originating in the Hebrew Bible (also known as the Tanakh) and explored in later texts such as the Talmud, Judaism is considered by religious Jews to be the expression of the covenantal relationship God developed with the Children of Israel. Rabbinic Judaism holds that

God revealed his laws and commandments to Moses on Mount Sinai in the form of both the Written and Oral Torah.

An assumed name; otherwise; at another time - Alias
    Example: "This author uses an alias for his books of poetry."

As much again; twice as much - Alterum tantum
    Example: "Sometimes fines are alterum tantum in places where there is work in progress."

At will; arbitrarily; at pleasure - Ad arbitrium
    Example: "Only dictators can act ad arbitrium."

Balzac: A good husband is never the first to go to sleep at night or the last to awake in the morning. (Honoré de Balzac)

Balzac: Children, dear and loving children, can alone console a woman for the loss of her beauty.

Balzac: Love has its own instinct, finding the way to the heart, as the feeblest insect finds the way to its flower, with a will which nothing can dismay nor turn aside.

Byron: I only go out to get me a fresh appetite for being alone. (Lord Byron - British Poet)

Churchill: I have taken more out of alcohol than alcohol has taken out of me.

Cicero: Breath; breeze; poetic inspiration - Afflatus
    Example: "In solving some difficult problems you need a lot of hard work, but also some afflatus."

Cicero: He has departed, absconded, escaped, disappeared – Abiit, excessit, evasit, erupit
    Example: "When you see that a man wants to really go away, you can say abiit, excessit, evasit, erupit."

Dediu: Happiness comes when you do good things for you, your family, your friends and many others.

Don't speak against the Sun (i.e., an obvious fact) - Adversus solem ne loquitor
    Example: "When somebody tries to explain obvious things, just say adversus solem ne loquitor."

Don't touch me; touch me not - Noli me tangere
    Example: "An aristocratic lady addressed to an young man with the classical noli me tangere."

Epicurus: Do not spoil what you have by desiring what you have not; remember that what you now have was once among the things you only hoped for.

Epicurus: Riches do not exhilarate us so much with their possession as they torment us with their loss.

For the sake of pleasing - Ad captandum
    Example: "Many politicians say certain things just ad captandum."

From another source; from outside, from elsewhere - Aliunde
    Example: "This information came aliunde and it is not reliable."

From one to all - Ab uno ad omnes
    Example: "When somebody has a good idea and all the others agree with that idea, we say ab uno ad omnes."

Here and everywhere - Hic et ubique
    Example: "All the scientific laws are valic hic et ubique."

Horace: Triple brass; a strong defense - Aes triplex
    Example: "This military unit has aes triplex."

Horace: A word once sent abroad flies irrevocably.

Horace: Leave the rest to the gods.

Horace: One wanders to the left, another to the right. Both are equally in error, but, are seduced by different delusions.

Latin maxims - Sententiae latinae
Example: "It is very beneficial and pleasant to often use sententiae latinae."

Mine and yours - Meum et tuum
Example: "Classical works, which are available for all, are meum et tuum."

O, come, all ye faithful - Adeste Fideles -.
Example: "It is so beautiful this hymn Adeste Fideles."

Of a different class - Alieni generis
Example: "The current project is alieni generis compared to the previous project."

Otherwise called, also known as, aka - Alias dictus
Example: "Richard, alias dictus Bobby, was a good chemist."

Ovid: **To feed the flames** - Alere flammam
  Example: "It is important alere flammam of liberty and hard work ubiquitously."

Ovid: Happy is the man who has broken the chains which hurt the mind, and has given up worrying once and for all.

Ovid: Everyone's a millionaire where promises are concerned.

Ovid: Beauty is a fragile gift.

Ovid: In our leisure we reveal what kind of people we are.

Ovid: The lamp burns bright when wick and oil are clean.

Ovid: What is it that love does to a woman? Without, she only sleeps; with it alone, she lives.

Ovid: Whether they give or refuse, it delights women just the same to have been asked.

Ovid: Why should I go into details, we have nothing that is not perishable except what our hearts and our intellects endows us with.

Plato: All the gold which is under or upon the earth is not enough to give in exchange for virtue.

Plato: At the touch of love everyone becomes a poet.

Plato: Love is the joy of the good, the wonder of the wise, the amazement of the Gods.

Plato: Music is a moral law. It gives soul to the universe, wings to the mind, flight to the imagination, and charm and gaiety to life and to everything.

Plato: Poets utter great and wise things which they do not themselves understand.

Plato: Then not only an old man, but also a drunkard, becomes a second time a child.

Plato: This City is what it is because our citizens are what they are.

Plato: Wise men speak because they have something to say; Fools because they have to say something.

Room for doubt - Ambigendi locus
    Example: "When they examined all the details of that problem, there was plenty of ambigendi locus."

Rousseau: God made me and broke the mold. (Jean-Jacques Rousseau - Philosopher)

Rousseau: I may be no better, but at least I am different.

Rousseau: Happiness: a good bank account, a good cook, and a good digestion.

Something bitter; a touch of bitterness - Amari aliquid
    Example: "On a very sweet chocolate it is nice to add amari aliquid."

Something; somewhat - Aliquid
    Example: "Observing aliquid abnormal on the computer screen, he asked a specialist for help."

That which is built - Aedificatum
   Example: "This new building here looks like aedificatum over there."

The fire within - Ignis internum
   Example: "For many artists, ignis internum is essential for creating new works.

To faith - Ad fidem
   Example: "Many apostolic letters refer ad fidem."

To mark the day with a white stone - Albo lapillo notare diem
   Example: "This is a happy day, therefore we want albo lapillo notare diem."

To or for whom; to or for which - Ad quem
   Example: "The managed set a day ad quem this project must be finished."

To the clergy - Ad clerum
Example: "When a church leader wants to address only to the clergy, he says ad clerum."

To the outside - Ad extra
Example: "We usually talk to our team, but occasionally we need to address ad extra."

To the center of the road - Ad filum viae
Example: "The local Land Registry applies the principle of ad filum viae to determine the ownership of the land."

To the effect - Ad effectum
Example: "The engineer explained this technical process ad effectum."

To the purse. (i.e., appealing to self-interest) - Ad crumenam
Example: "Many salesmen continuously speak ad crumenam."

To the same degree (i.e., equal blame or praise) - Ad eundem gradum
Example: "This student from a local university asked to be admitted ad eundem gradum to another university."

To this word - Ad hanc vocem
Example: "Mark noted that these words appear to be related ad hanc vocem."

Twain: I must have a prodigious quantity of mind; it takes me as much as a week sometimes to make it up. (Mark Twain)

Virgil: I recognize the signs of the old flame - Agnosco
veteris vestigia flammae
    Example: "This man tells his wife about his love for
her: agnosco veteris vestigia flammae."

What we obtain by asking is not really ours - Alienum est
omne quicquid optando evenit
    Example: "If you receive something by asking,
remember that alienum est omne quicquid optando evenit."

White - Albus
    Example: "The albus snow is all over the land."

White book – Liber albus
    Example: "There is a Liber albus of the City of
London."

Chapter I. 8 - Science

A wise man states as true nothing he does not prove - Sapiens nihil affirmat quod non probat

 Example: "Proving is the fundamental rule of science, therefore sapiens nihil affirmat quod non probat."

According to a rule (i.e., with precision, accurately) - Ad amussim

 Example: "This software development project was done ad amussim."

An uneven part of the whole - Aliquant

 Example: "In mathematics, when a number n1 is not a divisor of another number n2, we say n1 is an aliquant part of n2, e.g. 7 is an aliquant part of 19."

An unknown land - Tera incognita

 Example: "There are still parts of the Earth which are tera incognita."

Archimedes: Give me a lever long enough and a fulcrum on which to place it, and I shall move the world. (Archimedes – Mathematician)

Balzac: It is the mark of a great man that he puts to flight all ordinary calculations. He is at once sublime and touching, childlike and of the race of giants. (Honoré de Balzac)

Dediu: - Creativity comes from observation, knowledge and thinking at square.

Dediu: - Innovation is applied creativity.

Dediu: - Mathematical algorithms and camera technology will make better global positioning systems (GPS).

Dediu: - Science and technology are the engines of progress.

Dediu: - The Internet is like a huge library – keep it clean and unpolluted.

Dediu: - The space and time are infinite.

Equal parts - Aequales
    Example: "The students are working on a problem to divide a circle in 7 aequales."

Euler: Nothing at all takes place in the universe in which some rule of maximum or minimum does not appear. (Leonhard Euler- Mathematician)

Fermi: There are two possible outcomes: if the result confirms the hypothesis, then you've made a measurement. If the result is contrary to the hypothesis, then you've made a discovery. (Enrico Fermi)

Fermi: Before I came here I was confused about this subject. Having listened to your lecture I am still confused. But on a higher level.

Fermi: If I could remember the names of all these particles, I'd be a botanist.

Fermi: Ignorance is never better than knowledge.

Fermi: It is no good to try to stop knowledge from going forward.)

From the maximum to the minimum - A maximis ad minima
 Example: "Whatever is the intensity of your work, a maximis ad minima, always pay attention to quality."

From the sky to the center of the earth - A caelo usque ad centrum
 Example: "In the Roman times, an owner owned everything a caelo usque ad centrum, but these days we have airplanes, oil exploration under your house, etc."

Horace: Nature can be expelled with a fork, but nevertheless always returns - Naturam expellas furca, tamen usque recurret
 Example: "When you take the basic nature of everything into account, you notice that naturam expellas furca, tamen usque recurret."

Maxwell: Ampere was the Newton of Electricity. (James M. Maxwell)

Maxwell: All the mathematical sciences are founded on relations between physical laws and laws of numbers, so that the aim of exact science is to reduce the problems of nature to the determination of quantities by operations with numbers.

Nature abhors a vacuum - Natura abhorret a vacuo
   Example: "Before the discovery of the atmospheric pressure, the pseudo-explanation, for why a liquid will climb up a tube to fill a vacuum, was natura abhorret a vacuo.

Newton: Nature is exceedingly simple and harmonious with itself - Natura valde simplex est et sibi consona
   Example: "The nature is extremely complex, but seen from a particular point of view, like Newton's, natura valde simplex est et sibi consona."

Plato: Astronomy compels the soul to look upwards and leads us from this world to another.

Plato: We ought to fly away from earth to heaven as quickly as we can; and to fly away is to become like God, as far as this is possible; and to become like him is to become holy, just, and wise.

Poincare: A small error in the former will produce an enormous error in the latter. (Henri Poincare – Mathematician)

Poincare: It is through science that we prove, but through intuition that we discover.
Poincare: Science is made of facts.

Poincare: Hypotheses are what we lack the least.

Poincare: In the old days when people invented a new function, they had something useful in mind.

Poincare: Mathematical discoveries, small or great, are never born of spontaneous generation.
Poincare: Mathematicians are born, not made.

Poincare: Mathematicians do not study objects, but relations between objects.

Poincare: The scientist does not study nature because it is useful; he studies it because he delights in it, and he delights in it because it is beautiful.

Poincare: Thought is only a flash between two long nights, but this flash is everything.

Poincare: To doubt everything, or, to believe everything, are two equally convenient solutions; both dispense with the necessity of reflection.

Poincare: One would have to have completely forgotten the history of science, so as to not remember that the desire to know nature has had the most constant and the happiest influence on the development of mathematics.

Poincare: It is far better to foresee even without certainty, than not to foresee at all.

Seneca: There is no easy way from the earth to the stars - Non est ad astra mollis e terris via
> *Example*: "As we so clearly saw from the space exploration, non est ad astra mollis e terris via

State of exact balance between two actions - Aequilibrium indifferentiae
> *Example:* "There are many studies in physics related to the aequilibrium indifferentiae."

To ignorance [of the facts of an argument] - Ad ignorantiam
> *Example:* "He cannot use an appeal ad ignorantiam, because he knew all the facts of this problem."

To the absurd - Ad absurdum
> *Example:* "In mathematics, the method of proof by reductio ad absurdum is very useful and important."

To the starts - Ad astra
> *Example:* "We should make every effort to explore other planets, and to go ad astra."

Chapter I. 9 - History

Always faithful - Semper fidelis
Example: "The official motto from 1883 and the marching song of the United States Marine Corps is Semper Fidelis."

Always ready - Semper paratus
Example: "The official motto and the marching song of the United States Coast Guard is Semper Paratus."

Attached to the soil; a serf - Adscriptus glebae -
Example: "In feudal days, like in Russia until 1861, a laborer, which was adscriptus glebae, could be sold with the land."

Balzac: Power is action; the electoral principle is discussion. No political action is possible when discussion is permanently established. (Honoré de Balzac)

Balzac: Power is not revealed by striking hard or often, but by striking true.

By force and arms - Vi et armis
      Example: "When somebody tries to persuade vi et armis, it may be necessary to respond in the same way."

Byron: I have no consistency, except in politics; and that probably arises from my indifference to the subject altogether. (Lord Byron - British Poet)

Calvin Coolidge - *"It is accordance with our determination to refrain from aggression and build up a sentiment and practice among nations more favorable to peace...that we have incurred the consent of fourteen important nations to the negotiations of a treaty condemning recourse to war, renouncing it as an instrument of national policy." Calvin Coolidge (1872-1933), U.S president. New York Times (August 16, 1928)*

Churchill: A joke is a very serious thing.

Churchill: A lie gets halfway around the world before the truth has a chance to get its pants on.

Churchill: A man does what he must - in spite of personal consequences, in spite of obstacles and dangers and pressures - and that is the basis of all human morality.

Churchill: A pessimist sees the difficulty in every opportunity; an optimist sees the opportunity in every difficulty.

Churchill: A politician needs the ability to foretell what is going to happen tomorrow, next week, next month, and next year. And to have the ability afterwards to explain why it didn't happen.

Churchill: All the great things are simple, and many can be expressed in a single word: freedom, justice, honor, duty, mercy, hope.

Churchill: I have been brought up and trained to have the utmost contempt for people who get drunk.

Churchill: I have never developed indigestion from eating my words.

Churchill: I have nothing to offer but blood, toil, tears and sweat.

Churchill: Courage is what it takes to stand up and speak; courage is also what it takes to sit down and listen.

Churchill: Although personally I am quite content with existing explosives, I feel we must not stand in the path of improvement.

Cicero : The welfare of the people is to be the highest law - Salus populi suprema lex esto

Dediu: In capitalism everybody complains that men exploit men. In communism and socialism is vice-versa, but everybody applauds, when directed.

Dediu: Television should be a tool for learning and good entertainment, not for bad propaganda.

Epicurus: A free life cannot acquire many possessions, because this is not easy to do without servility to mobs or monarchs.

Epicurus: I have never wished to cater to the crowd; for what I know they do not approve, and what they approve I do not know.

Epicurus: The greater the difficulty, the more the glory in surmounting it.

Flavius: - If you want peace, prepare for war - Si vis pacem, para bellum (Publius Flavius Vegetius Renatus)

For the perpetual remembrance of the thing - Ad perpetuam rei memoriam
    Example: "On some official documents of the church it is written ad perpetuam rei memoriam."

From God and the king - A Deo et rege
    Example: "The kings used the expression a Deo et rege to impose their will on the people."

From the spear a crown - A cuspide corona
    Example: "Many times in the past, the kings got their crowns by spears and wars, therefore a cuspide corona."

Horace: A shoe that is too large is apt to trip one, and when too small, to pinch the feet. So it is with those whose fortune does not suit them.

Horace: Every old poem is sacred.

Horace: He has not lived badly, whose birth and death has been unnoticed by the world.

It is all over with the republic - Actum est de re publica
    Example: "When the people of a country do not pay enough attention to the military defense, an enemy will

attack and occupy the country, and then actum est de re publica."

Julius Caesar: I came, I saw, I conquered - Veni vidi vici
   Example: "In 47 B.C. Julius Caesar sent the laconic dispatch veni vidi vici to the Senate, regarding his victory over Pharnaces, king of Pontus."

Julius Caesar: The die is cast. - Alea iacta est
   Example: "Julius Caesar, having made the decision to cross the river Rubicon on January 10, 49 BC, to begin a war against Pompey, said: alea iacta est."

Hoover: All men are equal before fish. *(Herbert Hoover, the 31ˢᵗ President of the United States (1929 – 1933))*

Napoleon: Imagination rules the world.

Napoleon: Impossible is a word to be found only in the dictionary of fools.

Napoleon: Music is the voice that tells us that the human race is greater than it knows.

Napoleon: Never interrupt your enemy when he is making a mistake.

Napoleon: Power is my mistress. I have worked too hard at her conquest to allow anyone to take her away from me.

Napoleon: Public opinion is the thermometer a monarch should constantly consult.

Napoleon: Skepticism is a virtue in history as well as in philosophy.

Napoleon: The French complain of everything, and always.

Ovid: Daring is not safe against daring men.

Ovid: Fortune and love favor the brave.

Ovid: Happy are those who dare courageously to defend what they love.

Ovid: Men do not value a good deed unless it brings a reward.

Ovid: A prince should be slow to punish, and quick to reward.

Ovid: People are slow to claim confidence in undertakings of magnitude.

Ovid: Tears at times have the weight of speech...

Ovid: The heavier crop is ever in others' fields.

Ovid: The vulgar crowd values friends according to their usefulness.

Plato: A state arises, as I conceive, out of the needs of mankind; no one is self-sufficing, but all of us have many wants.

Plato: Courage is knowing what not to fear.

Plato: Democracy passes into despotism.

Plato: Democracy... is a charming form of government, full of variety and disorder; and dispensing a sort of equality to equals and unequals alike.

Plato: Dictatorship naturally arises out of democracy, and the most aggravated form of tyranny and slavery out of the most extreme liberty.

Plato: Excess generally causes reaction, and produces a change in the opposite direction, whether it be in the seasons, or in individuals, or in governments.

Plato: Excess of liberty, whether it lies in state or individuals seems only to pass into excess of slavery.

Plato: For the introduction of a new kind of music must be shunned as imperiling the whole state; since styles of music are never disturbed without affecting the most important political institutions.

Plato: Good actions give strength to ourselves and inspire good actions in others.

Plato: He who is not a good servant will not be a good master.

Plato: No one ever teaches well, who wants to teach, or governs well, who wants to govern.

Plato: One of the penalties for refusing to participate in politics is that you end up being governed by your inferiors.

Plato: Only the dead have seen the end of war.

Plato: Our object in the construction of the state is the greatest happiness of the whole, and not that of any one class.

Plato: Rhetoric is the art of ruling the minds of men.

Plato: States are as the men, they grow out of human characters.

Plato: The curse of me and my nation is that we always think things can be bettered by immediate action of some sort, any sort rather than no sort.

Plato: The measure of a man is what he does with power.

Plato: The most virtuous are those who content themselves with being virtuous without seeking to appear so.

Plato: The punishments which the wise suffer, who refuse to take part in the government, is to live under the government of worse men.

Plato: The rulers of the state are the only persons who ought to have the privilege of lying, either at home or abroad; they may be allowed to lie for the good of the state.

Plato: The wisest have the most authority.

Plato: There will be no end to the troubles of states, or of humanity itself, till philosophers become kings in this world, or till those we now call kings and rulers really and truly become philosophers, and political power and philosophy thus come into the same hands.

Plato: This and no other is the root from which a tyrant springs; when he first appears he is a protector.

Plato: We are twice armed if we fight with faith.

Plato: When the tyrant has disposed of foreign enemies by conquest or treaty, and there is nothing more to fear from them, then he is always stirring up some war or other, in order that the people may require a leader.

Plato: When there is an income tax, the just man will pay more and the unjust less on the same amount of income.

Reagan: Information is the oxygen of the modern age. It seeps through the walls topped by barbed wire; it wafts across the electrified borders. (Ronald Reagan – U.S. President)

Reagan: It's true hard work never killed anybody, but I figure, why take the chance?

Reagan: No matter what time it is, wake me, even if it's in the middle of a Cabinet meeting.

To capture the crowd - Ad captandum vulgus
    Example: "Many things are done in this world just ad captandum vulgus."

To the stick (i.e., appeal to force, not reason) - Ad baculum
    Example: "Unfortunately there are still countries where the main argument is ad baculum."

Chapter I. 10 - Medical

Above all do no harm; first do not harm - Primum non nocere

    Example: "All the medical doctors have to take the Hippocratic Oath, which contains, as a fundamental medical dictum, primum non nocere."

Balzac: Chance, my dear, is the sovereign deity in childbearing. (Honoré de Balzac)

Balzac: It is only in the act of nursing that a woman realizes her motherhood in visible and tangible fashion; it is a joy of every moment.

Balzac: What is a child, monsieur, but the image of two beings, the fruit of two sentiments spontaneously blended?

Balzac: Love is the poetry of the senses.

Byron: It is very certain that the desire of life prolongs it. (Lord Byron - British Poet)

Dediu: Life and death are interrelated, they cannot exist without each other, but the life should have much more time to be around, and here the medical assistance is vital.

Edison: The chief function of the body is to carry the brain around.

For external use - Ad usum externum
    Example: "There are many medicines which are only ad usum externum."

He is sick - Aegrotat
    Example: "In British universities, if some students are too sick to pass an examination, then each obtains an aegrotat."

Horace: Remember to maintain a calm mind while doing difficult tasks - Aequam memento rebus in arduis servare mentem
    Example: "The manager used to tell his team: aequam memento rebus in arduis servare mentem."

Horace: To preserve a calm mind; equanimity - Aequam servare mentem
    Example: "In difficult situations it is imperative aequam servare mentem."

Horace: Anger is a short madness.

Horace: Subdue your passion or it will subdue you.

In the absence of fever - Absente febre
    Example: "His influenza developed absente febre."

Juvenal: A sound mind in a sound body - Mens sana in corpore sano

Example: "It is a perpetual desire for everybody to have mens sana in corpore sano."

Napoleon: The best cure for the body is a quiet mind.

Not of sound mind - Non compus mentis
    Example: "The medical doctors have to determine if a person is non compos mentis."

Not to injure other - Alterum non laedere
    Example: "A very important rule in any human activity is alterum non laedere."

Ovid: Like fragile ice, anger passes away in time.

Ovid: Ah me! love cannot be cured by herbs.

Ovid: There is more refreshment and stimulation in a nap, even of the briefest, than in all the alcohol ever distilled.

Ovid: There is no such thing as pure pleasure; some anxiety always goes with it.

Ovid: Time is generally the best doctor.

Ovid: Suppressed grief suffocates, it rages within the breast, and is forced to multiply its strength.

Ovid: Take rest; a field that has rested gives a beautiful crop.

Ovid: The cause is hidden; the effect is visible to all.

Ovid: To feel our ills is one thing, but to cure them is another.

Ovid: What is without periods of rest will not endure.

Plato: Attention to health is life's greatest hindrance.

Rousseau: Our affections as well as our bodies are in perpetual flux. (Jean-Jacques Rousseau - Philosopher)

Shake before taking - Agita nate sumendum
  Example: "On many bottles with liquid medicines it is written agita nate sumendum."

Sick; ill - Aeger
  Example: "In British universities the students use aeger as a medical excuse."

To the life - Ad vivum
  Example: "The best ad vivum anesthesiology can be found in many good hospitals."

To the painful parts - Ad partes dolentes
  Example: "Special medication was applied ad partes dolentes."

Virgil: A sick man's dream; hallucination - Aegri somnia vana
  Example: "When a patient has high fever, a consequence could be aegri somnia vana."

Virgil: Nursing an everlasting wound within the breast - Aeternum servans sub pectore vulnus

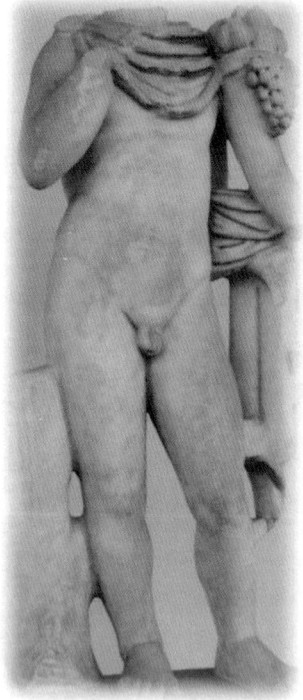

Example: "When there is a big disappointment, we feel like aeternum servans sub pectore vulnus."

Virgil: The disease worsens with the treatment - Aegrescit medendo
   Example: "Until recently, the medical treatment was not very scientific, and, sometimes, aegrescit medendo."

When the fever increases - Aggrediente febre
   Example: "In this case, there are special medical procedures aggrediente febre."

When fever is present - Adstante febre
   Example: "In this case, a different medical instruction is given adstante febre."

With a calm mind; with equanimity - Aequo animo
   Example: "I observed him working, in very stressful situations, aequo animo."

With composure; with equanimity; imperturbability - Aequanimitas
   Example: "One of the most important requirements for physicians is aequanimitas."

PART II Latin

Chapter II. 1 – Philosophy

Abscisio infiniti - Cutting off an infinite part
This expression is used when a long speech or explanation must be stopped.

    Example: when somebody is talking ad infinitum, kindly suggest: "Nice talk, but please use the abscisio infiniti."

Ad Limina Apostolorum - To the thresholds of the apostles
This is an ecclesiastical expression meaning a pilgrimage to the tombs of the Apostles St. Peter and St. Paul at Rome, Italy.

    Example: "When we'll go to Rome, let's visit, like the bishops, Limina Apostolorum."

Ad nocendum patentes sumus -We all have power to do harm (Seneca)

    Example: "Even if ad nocendum patentes sumus, we should always try not to do harm."

Ad praesens ova cras pullis sunt meliora- Eggs today are better than chickens tomorrow.
Example: "If we have a crisis now, then ad praesens ova cras pullis sunt meliora."

Aliquando bonus dormitat Homerus - Sometimes even good Homer sleeps.
It is used to express forgiveness of a work which is not very good.

    Example: "This book is good, but the last chapter, well, aliquando bonus dormitat Homerus".

Aliquis in omnibus, nullus in singulis - A somebody in general, a nobody in particular.
For somebody who knows many general things, but is no expert in anything.
    Example: "John read several books, but he is still aliquis in omnibus, nullus in singulis."

Alitur vitium vivitque tegendo - Vice is nourished by being concealed.
    Example: "In a company it is better to report corruption, immorality and other vices, otherwise alitur vitium vivitque tegendo."

Alteri sic tibi - [Do] to another as [you do] to yourself.
    Example: "In a civilized society, everybody should act thinking first that alteri sic tibi."

Altissima quaeque flumina minimo sono labiuntur - The deepest rivers flow with the least sound.
    Example: "In this discussion in a group of people, that professor is much quieter than the others around, because altissima quaeque flumina minimo sono labiuntur"

Amabit sapiens, cupient caeteri - Wise men love, others are mere lechers.
Example: "Analyzing history, it is easy to observe that amabit sapiens, cupient caeteri."

Amans iratus multa mentitur sibi - An angry lover tells himself many lies.
    Example: "John loves Mary, but they had a small conflict, and John began to say many strange things; then I told him amans iratus multa mentitur sibi."

Amantes sunt amentes - Lovers are lunatics. (Terence)
    Example: "Love creates a lot of exuberance, and we can jokingly say that amantes sunt amentes."

Amantium irae amoris integratio est – The anger of lovers is the renewal of love. (Terence)
    Example: "Seeing Ron and July having a little dispute, I reminded them that amantium irae amoris integratio est."

Bis vivit qui bene vivit – He lives twice who lives well
    Example: "One who lives well from all points of view, will easily notice that bis vivit qui bene vivit."

Bonitas non est pessimis esse meliorem - It is not goodness to be better than the worst.
    Example: "When Sam told his father that he is not the worst in his class, the father told him that bonitas non est pessimis esse meliorem."

Ecce homo - behold the man.
    Example: "There are many religious paintings and sculptures with the title ecce homo."

Eheu! fugaces labuntur anni – Alas! The fleeting years are passing. (Horace)

    Example: "After a number of years, everybody will nostalgically say like Horace: Eheu! fugaces labuntur anni!"

Errare humanum est, perseverare diabolicum - To err is human, to persevere is of the devil.

    Example: "Now and then, the parents have to remind their children that errare humanum est, perseverare diabolicum."

Fabas indulcet fames - Hunger sweetens the beans.

    Example: "Peter did not like much the beans, but after some dire experiences, he was very hungry and noticed that fabas indulcet fames".

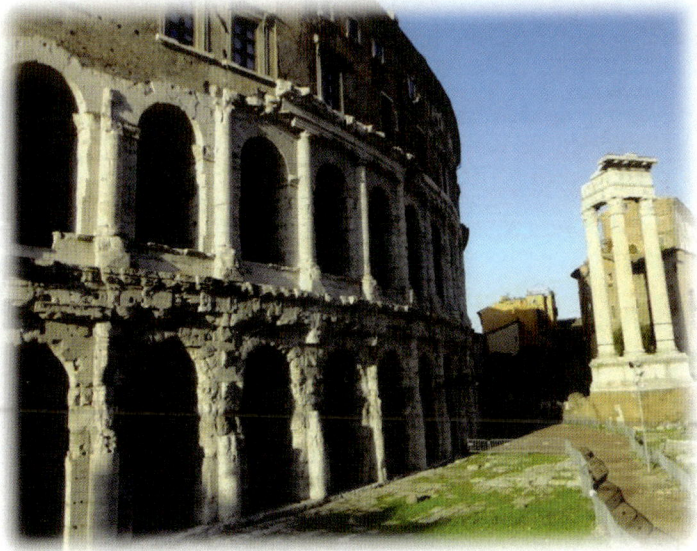

Facta non verba - Deeds, not words.

Example: "Many times we notice that people, especially politicians and salesmen, promise a lot, but do not deliver; then let's tell them facta non verba!"

Fallaces sunt rerum species et hominum spes fallunt - The appearances of things are deceptive and the hope of men is deceived. (Seneca)
Example: "So frequently, unfortunately, especially in astronomy, what we see is not what we hoped and we have to repeat after Seneca: fallaces sunt rerum species et hominum spes fallunt."

Fiat justitia ruat caelum - Let justice be done through the heavens fall.
Example: "It is important to have justice for all, and if someone asks to be excepted, the response should be fiat justitia ruat caelum."

In pace, ut sapiens, aptarit idonea bello - In peace, as a wise man, he appropriately prepares for war. (Horace)
Example: "It is very unfortunate, but, if we look what happens in the world, we must agree with Horace: in pace, ut sapiens, aptarit idonea bello."

In vino veritas - In wine there is truth.
Example: "Drinking some wine gives more willingness to say the truth, therefore we can say in vino veritas".

Mutantur omnia nos et mutamur in illis - All things change, and we change with them.
Example: "With the passing of the years, we begin to notice that mutantur omnia nos et mutamur in illis."

Memento mori - Remember that you will die.

Example: "There are some people who feel so powerful and dominant forever that it is good to be reminded this simple truth: memento mori."

Mendacem memorem esse oportet (Quintilianus) - A liar needs a good memory.
Example: "In politics especially, where the lies are not unusual, it is easy to observe that mendacem memorem esse oportet."

Mens agitat molem – Mind drives matter (Virgil)
Example: "Many changes around us were produced as result of some initial ideas and plans, therefore mens agitat molem".

Mens rea – Guilty mind.
Example: "Many bad things happen because of this mens rea."

Minima maxima sunt - The smallest things are most important.
Example: "In life, let's not forget, minima maxima sunt."

Multum in parvo - Much in little.
Example: "This multum in parvo is often used under the acronym form MIP, and it appears for example in computer technology as mipmaps, which need more space in memory."

Mutatis mutandis - With the necessary changes.
Example: "The current situation, mutatis mutandis, can become much better for all."

Ne quid nimis – Not anything in excess.

Example: "One of the fundamental rules of a good life is ne quid nimis."

Nemo dat quod non habet - No one gives what he does not have.
Example: "When somebody tries to sell or give something which he does not possess, he should be advised that nemo dat quod non habet."

Nemo liber est qui corpori servit - No one is free who is a slave to his body.
Example: "Those who are obsessed with taking care only of their bodies, not of their intellect, will shortly discover the truth that nemo liber est qui corpori servit."

Non est ad astra mollis e terris via (Seneca)- There is no easy way from the earth to the stars.
Example: "As we so clearly saw from the space exploration, non est ad astra mollis e terris via."

Non est vivere sed valere vita est - Life is not being alive but being well.
Example: "It is not sufficient to just be alive, you have to be well and do many other things, therefore non est vivere sed valere vita est."

Non semper erit aestas - It will not always be summer (be prepared for hard times).
Example: "Be ready for difficult times, because non semper erit aestas."

Non teneas aurum totum quod splendet ut aurum - Do not take as gold everything that shines like gold.
Example: "Shakespeare's "All that glitters is not gold" remind us of non teneas aurum totum quod splendet ut aurum."

Nosce te ipsum - Know thyself.
Example: "Before you want to know many other things, nosce te ipsum."

O passi gravoria, dabit deus his quoque finem – Oh, suffering ones, God will grant an end to these things too. (Virgil)
Example: "Seeing the consequences of an earthquake, an old man said o passi gravoria, dabit deus his quoque finem".

Omnia causa fiunt - Everything happens for a reason.
Example: "An important part of our research work, knowing that omnia causa fiunt, is to find causa (the reason."

Omnia mutantur, nihil interit (Ovid) - All things change, nothing perishes.
Example: "Looking carefully around, one can easily observe that omnia mutantur, nihil interit."

Omnia mutantur nos et mutamur in illis - All things change, and we change with them.
Example: "The life quickly teaches us that omnia mutantur nos et mutamur in illis."

Parva leves capiunt animas - Small things occupy light minds
Example: "The difficult problems in the world occupy the minds of great people, and parva leves capiunt animas."

Perfer et obdura; dolor hic tibi proderit olim (Ovid) - Be patient and tough; someday this pain will be useful to you.
Example: "There are many painful experiences in life, but perfer et obdura; dolor hic tibi proderit olim."

Periculum in mora – There is danger in delay
Example: "Especially in the justice system, but also in general, periculum in mora."

Proprium humani ingenii est odisse quem laeseris - It is human nature to hate a person whom you have injured.
Example: "It is not good at all, and it should be corrected, but proprium humani ingenii est odisse quem laeseris."

Qui vivat atque floreat ad plurimos annos – May he live and flourish for many years
Example: "In addition to "Happy Birthday!" we can say qui vivat atque floreat ad plurimos annos."

Quis custodiet ipsos custodes? - Who will watch the watchers themselves?
Example: "Sometimes we have so many regulators, guards, inspectors and warchers all around us, that we have to ask quis custodiet ipsos custodes?

Radix malorum est cupiditas - The root of evil is greed. Avarice is the problem, money itself is not evil.

Example: "Money itself is a necessity, and, of course it is not evil, but for avarice and greed we can say radix malorum est cupiditas."

Respice, adspice, prospice - Look back, look at the present, look ahead

Example: "The definition of history as being like a lamp from the past, turned on in the present, to light the future, was inspired by respice, adspice, prospice."

Sedit qui timuit ne non succederet (Horace). – He, who feared he would not succeed, sat still.

Example: "In order to succeed one needs to be very active and motivated, otherwise we apply this: sedit qui timuit ne non succederet."

Sic transit gloria mundi - Thus passes away earthly glory

Example: "Many oppressive and violent dictators were finally taken out, and then the eliberated people could say sic transit gloria mundi."

Sic vis pacem para bellum - If you wish for peace, prepare for war.

Example: "It is very unfortunate, indeed, but the history always proved it, therefore everybody should understand that sic vis pacem para bellum."

Timendi causa est nescire (Seneca)- The cause of fear is ignorance

Example: "The more we know, the better we understand, because timendi causa est nescire."

Ut sementem feceris ita metes - As you sow, so shall you reap.

Example: "It is very important to teach the children that ut sementem feceris ita metes."

Varium et mutabile semper femina (Virgil) – Woman is always a changeable and capricious thing
Example: "Giuseppe Verdi in "La donna e mobile", from his opera Rigoletto, uses this Virgil's comment varium et mutabile semper femina."

Verbum sat sapienti - A word is sufficient for a wise man.
Example: "In many critical situations, only one proper word can make the difference between a good or bad output, but it is very difficult to find somebody who knows that proper word, for this we say verbum sat sapienti."

Veritas vos liberabit - The truth shall set you free
Example: "Those who lie too much become the prisoniers of their own lies, and they should be reminded that veritas vos liberabit."

Vincit qui se vincit - He conquers who conquers himself.
Example: "One, who has a strong auto-control and self-discipline, has a better chance to achive great results, therefore vincit qui se vincit."

Vita non est vivere sed valere vita est – Life is not being alive but being well

 Example: "A meaningful life is, certainly, more than merely staying alive, therefore vita non est vivere sed valere vita est."

Vir sapit qui pauca loquitur – It is a wise man who speaks little

 Example: "Somebody, who can use just a few words to describe a complex situation, is very capable, therefore vir sapit qui pauca loquitur."

Vox populi vox dei - The voice of the people is the voice of God.

 Example: "Even when the people are oppressed by brutal dictators, after some time, the voice of the people will be heard, because vox populi vox dei."

Chapter II. 2 - Success

Acerbus et ingens - Fierce and mighty.
　　　Example: "For success one needs to be acerbus et ingens."

Ad astra per aspera - To the stars through difficulties.
　　　Example: "Is it easy to be successful? Well, ad astra per aspera."

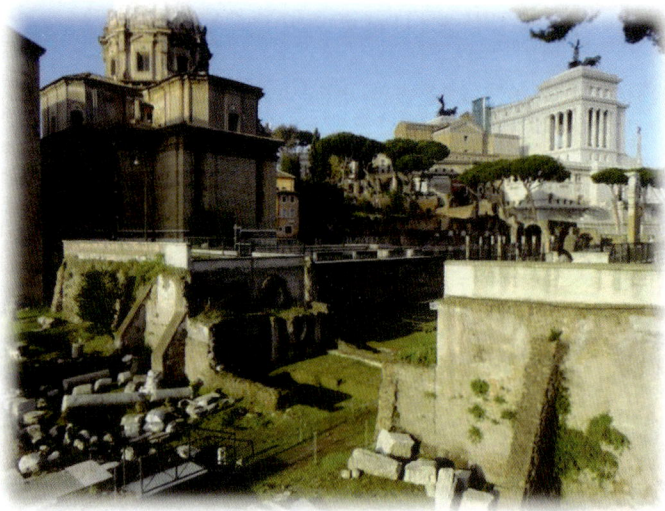

Ad gloriam - For the glory.
　　　Example: "Many artists work hard ad gloriam."

Adversa virtute repello - I repel adversity by valor.
　　　Example: "Unfortunately, there is much adversity in the world, but everybody should say adversa virtute repello".

Altiora peto - I seek higher things.

Example: "If success is the objective, then you should always say altiora peto."

Aut viam inveniam aut faciam - I'll either find a way or make one.
Example: "Great commanders and achievers many times say aut viam inveniam aut faciam."

Laborare est orare – To work is to pray
Example: "For many great achievers, laborare est orare."

Modus operandi – Mode of operation
Example: "Anybody who works for achieving a certain result needs a modus operandi."

Modus vivendi - A mode of living.
Example: "A very important issue in life is to find modus vivendi."

Non est ad astra mollis e terris via (Seneca) - There is no easy way from the earth to the stars.
Example: "Sooner or later everybody find out that non est ad astra mollis e terris via."

Nulli secundus - Second to none
Example: "Our team is nulli secundus."

Per aspera ad astra! - Through difficulties to the stars!
Example: "How do we achieve great results? Per aspera ad astra!"

Here we have a nice poem too.

Per Aspera Ad Astra
(Through Difficulties To The Stars)
by
Michael M. Dediu

Per aspera ad astra
Said the Romans long ago.
Let a Universe orchestra,
Start a grand and cosmic show.

Study physics, mathematics,
Perdurable chemistry;
Then with bioastronautics,
See what's new in geometry.

Now nanotechnology
Is the future for the space.
Fly ad astra, use pomology,
To see, friend, moon's other face.

Sic itur ad astra means
Such's the way to stars.
Work to reach antipodeans

At the Universe altars.

Every breath you take,
Make it an abutment.
For the move you make,
To be an achievement.

Make the Universe gallant…
Learn much more than yesterday.
Dare be happy and more volant.
Make some progress every day!

Perfer et obdura; dolor hic tibi proderit olim (Ovid) - Be patient and tough; someday this pain will be useful to you. *Example*: "To be successful you'll have to pass through some painful situations, but perfer et obdura; dolor hic tibi proderit olim."

Possunt quia posse videntur (Virgil) - They can because they think they can
    Example: "Looking at big achievers, Virgil's words come to mind: Possunt quia posse videntur."

Qui audet adipiscitur - Who dares wins
    Example: "You need to dare, because only qui audet adipiscitur."

Sedit qui timuit ne non succederet (Horace) - He who feared that he would not succeed sat still.
    Example: "Move ahead, because only sedit qui timuit ne non succederet."

Sequere pecuniam - Follow the money

Si finis bonus est, totum bonum erit - If the end is good, everything will be good

Example: "After all the ups and downs, si finis bonus est, totum bonum erit."

Si quid novisti rectius istis, candidus imperti; si nil, his utere mecum (Horace) - If you can better these principles, tell me; if not, join me in following them
Example: "Refering to the ideas from this book: si quid novisti rectius istis, candidus imperti; si nil, his utere mecum."

Si vis amari, ama (Seneca) - If you want to be loved, love

Tu ne cede malis sed contra audentior ito - Yield not to misfortunes, but advance ever more boldly against them
Example: "Bad things happen, however tu ne cede malis sed contra audentior ito."

Vincit qui se vincit - He conquers who conquers himself.
Example: "First you need self-discipline and self-control, because vincit qui se vincit."

Chapter II. 3 - Time

A dato - From the date.
> *Example*: "We'll start the inspection a dato when the building is finished."

A die - From that day
> *Example*: "One day last year they had a great victory; a die they did not succeed anymore."

Ab aeterno - From eternity
> *Example*: "Our universe is ab aeterno."

Ab incunabulis - From the cradle
> *Example*: "This child appeared to be smart ab incunabulis."

Ab initio - From the beginning
> *Example*: "We have to start this analysis ab initio."

Ab Iove principium (Virgil) - From Jove is the beginning
It can be translated also: Let's start with Jupiter.
It is from Virgil, Eclogue III. The Eclogues is the first of the three major works, pastorals, of the Latin poet Virgil. He takes as his generic model the Greek Bucolica ("On care of cattle", poem in which shepherds converse). Literally it means to start from the most important person

(because Jupiter was considered the chief of the Gods), or from the most important thing.

This expression is used at the beginning of a debate or an exposure, signaling that we'll start with the most important, or the principal assertion.

Example: "We'll have our presentation ab Iove principium."

Ab origine - From the origin
Example: "To better understand this situation, we have to start ab origine."

Ab ovo - From the egg
Another translation can be "from the beginning".

The point of time or space at which anything begins. The act or process of bringing or being brought into being; a start. In the Ars Poetica (The Art of Poetry or On the Nature of Poetry), the Latin poet Horace praises Homer that in his Iliad he stated that the Troy war started from the Greek Achilles hero's anger and not **ab ovo**, that is not from the birth of Helen, who according to the legend was born from the Leda's egg. (Troy was a city, both factual and legendary, located in northwest Anatolia in what is now Turkey, southeast of the Dardanelles and beside Mount Ida. It is best known for being the setting of the Trojan War described in the Greek Epic Cycle and especially in the Iliad, one of the two epic poems attributed to Homer)

Example: "There is no sufficient time now to start ab ovo.

Ab ovo usque ad mala (Horace) - From the egg to the apples
Example: "When we want to describe something from the beginning to the end we'll say: let's discuss this subject ab ovo usque ad mala."

Ab urbe condita - From the foundation of the city (Rome)
Example: "This tradition here in Rome is ab urbe condita."

Acta est fabula, plaudite! **(Augustus Caesar)** - The play is over, applaud!
Example: "The last words of the Roman Emperor Augustus Cesar were: acta est fabula, plaudite!"

Actum agere - To do what has already been done
Example: "In this project there is a lot of repetition, waste of time, unnecessary work and labor in vain, because they have actum agere."

Actum ne agas - Do not redo that which has been done
Example: "In this software development task, please actum ne agas."

Ad alium diem - At another day.
Example: "The mathematical analysis of this subject was deferred ad alium diem."

Ad calendas Graecas - At the Greek calends (i.e., never, as Greeks did not have calends).

Example: "It looks like this work will be finished ad calendas Graecas."

Ad extremum - To the extreme (i.e., to the very end).
Example: "They want to continue their exploration of this territory ad extremum."

Ad finem - To the end; at the end of the page
Example: "Those people supported their team ad finem."

Ad infinitum - To infinity; without an end; without limit
Example: "There is no activity which can go ad infinitum."

Ad initium - At the beginning
Example: "In this presentation, ad initium, we'll give some preliminary information."

Ad interim - In the time between; in the meantime; for the time being; temporary
Example: "The management appointed an ad interim team of engineers to inspect the production problems."

Ad multos annos - To many years
Example: "At his birthday everybody wished him ad multos annos!"

Ad paucos dies - For a few days
Example: "After they were in vacation ad paucos dies in Rome, they returned very happy and ready for work."

Ad vitam - For life; for the duration of a person's life
Example: "Some honorific positions are given ad vitam."

Ad vitam aeternam - For eternal life; for all time
    Example: "This classical symphonic music is ad vitam aeternam."

Ad vitam aut culpam - For life or until a misdeed
    Example: "There are judges who are appointed ad vitam aut culpam."

Aere perennius - More durable than bronze; everlasting
    Example: "There are many aere perennius monuments in Rome."

Aetatis - At the age of
    Example: "He began to study advanced mathematics aetatis 17."

Aeternum vale - Farewell forever
    Example: "After many successful years of teaching, the professor decided to say aeternum vale."

Anno aetatis suae - In the year of his age
    Example: "The great ancient Roman poet Publius Vergilius Maro (Virgil) died anno 19 BC aetatis suae 49."

Anno Urbis Contitae (AUC) – The City (Rome) Foundation Year
    Example: "For Rome, by tradition, Anno Urbis Contitae (AUC) is set in 753 BC."

Caret initio et fine - It lacks a beginning and an end
    Example: "His presentation is good, but caret initio et fine."

Seculo seculorum – Forever and ever

Tempus fugit - Time flies
    Example: "*Example*: "With the age, one begins to notice that tempus fugit faster and faster…"

Chapter II. 4 - Education

À bon entendeur, salut! (French.) – Good listener, hello!
The significance of this expression is: who has ears to hear, hear or listen up. Purposely, the expression is used in original, to attract the audience's attention, with the understanding that there is much more to the matter which cannot be said completely.
    Example: "For now, I said enough! À bon entendeur, salut!"

Ad aperturam libri - At the opening of a book
Example: "It is nice to be careful and concentrated ad aperturam libri."

Ad augusta per angusta - To honor through difficulties
    Example: "The road to high places many times passes through narrow and difficult paths, and the same we can say ad augusta per angusta."

Addendum - Something to be added
    Example: "Many scientific and technical books need to add some explanations, and each of them uses an addendum."

Adeo in teneris consuescere multum est - It is imperative to be well trained in early youth. (Virgil)
   Example: "Any parent and grandparent should know that adeo in teneris consuescere multum est."

Adhibenda est in iocando moderatio - One should employ restraint in his jests. (Cicero)
   Example: "Listening to some of the unrestrained, immoral and uncivilized jests of these days, we all ask that everybody should respect Cicero's rule: adhibenda est in iocando moderatio."

Ad unguem factus homo (Horace) -A man accomplished to his fingertips
   Example: "That man has achieved very much in all directions, he is ad unguem factus homo."

Ad usum Delphini -For the Dauphin's use; expurgated
   Example: "When some texts are purified, to be used by young people, one can say these texts are ad usum Delphini."

Ad verbum - To the word; verbatim
   Example: "Please translate this letter ad verbum."

Adversus bonos mores - Against good morals
   Example: "Unfortunately, there are too many things these days, which are adversus bonos mores."

Acta Eruditorum – Acts of the scholars
Example: "For 100 years, between 1682 and 1782, Acta Eruditorum was the first scientific journal of the German lands, initially published in Leipzig."

Alma mater - Kind mother (old students about their university)

Example: "Many graduates from good universities remember with nostalgia their alma mater."

Assiduus usus uni rei deditus et ingenium et artem saepe vincit (M.Tullius Cicero) - Constant practice devoted to one subject often outdoes both intelligence and skill
    Example: "Many people who concentrated on a sigle subject, sooner or later noticed that assiduus usus uni rei deditus et ingenium et artem saepe vincit."

Aut disce aut discede - Either learn or leave
Example: "At that advanced school of mathematics, you aut disce aut discede."

Difficile est tenere quae acceperis nisi exerceas - It is difficult to retain what you may have learned, unless you practice it
    Example: "As the years pass by, we all notice that difficile est tenere quae acceperis nisi exerceas."

Diligentia maximum etiam mediocris ingeni subsidium Diligence is a very great help, even to a mediocre intelligence
    Example: "It is important for parents and teachers to cultivate industry and perseverance in children, because diligentia maximum etiam mediocris ingeni subsidium."

Docendo discimus - Teach in order to learn (we learn by teaching)
    Example: "If you really want to learn well a certain difficult subject, then docendo discimus."

Experientia docet - Experience teaches
    Example: "Even if you have many years of good schools, still experientia docet much more."

Gaudeamus igitur - So let us rejoice
    Example: "For more than 200 years, the oldest student song is Gaudeamus igitur."

Homines dum docent discunt - Men learn while they teach (Seneca)
Example: "Teaching is a great way of learning, because homines dum docent discunt."

Ipsa scientia potestas est - Knowledge itself is power
    Example: "If one does not know much, it is difficult to get power, because ipsa scientia potestas est."
Here we have to repeat our maxim:
    Few people know,
    How much you have to know,
    To know,
    How little you know.

Lapsus calami - Slip of the pen

Lapsus linguae - Slip of the tongue

Lapsus manus - Slip of the hand

Lapsus memoriae - Slip of memory

Magnum opus - A great work
    Example: "Usually the greatest masterpiece of a writer or a composer is called magnum opus."

Non mihi, non tibi, sed nobis - Not for me, not for you, but for us
    Example: "When an award is given to our team, the we can say that this award is non mihi, non tibi, sed nobis."

Nosce te ipsum - Know thyself

Qui scribit bis legit - He who writes reads twice
  Example: "One who wants to remember something that he was reading, it is recommended to write it, because qui scribit bis legit."

Repetitio est mater studiorum - Repetition is the mother of studies
  Example: "From the very young age everybody learns that repetitio est mater studiorum."

Silentium est aureum - Silence is golden

Tabula rasa - A blank tablet (about a student's mind)
  Example: "Before receiving the impressions gained from experience, the human mind, especially at birth, is tabula rasa."

Chapter II. 5 - Practical

Ab actu ad posse valet illatio -.From the past one can infer the future
    Example: "What has happened is always important, because ab actu ad posse valet illation."

A bene placito - At one's pleasure
    Example: "After a great effort to finish the software project, the engineer had some free time a bene placito."

Abeunt studia in mores (Ovid) - Studies change into habits
    Example: "Very good education is so important, because abeunt studia in mores."

Ab extra - From the outside
    Example: "That team has received significant help ab extra."

Ab imo pectore (Julius Caesar) - From the bottom of the chest (heart)
Example: "Julius Caesar used to address to his people with sincerity and ab imo pectore."

Ab intra - From within
    Example: "The energy and the desire for success must come ab intra."

Ab irato - From the angry man (i.e., unfair)
    Example: "This manager took some ab irato decisions, which are not good for his team."

Ab ove maiori discit arare minor - From the older ox the younger learns to plow

Example: "The older generation has to teach the younger one many practical things, because ab ove maiori discit arare minor."

Absentem laedit cum ebrio qui litigat – He who quarrels with a drunk, hurts an absentee
Example: "It is much better to help a drunk to go to an assistance center, and not to quarrel with him, because absentem laedit cum ebrio qui litigat."

Absit invidia – Envy absent (i.e., no offense intended)
Example: "The manager critiqued an engineer, but absit invidia."

Absit omen - May the omen be absent (i.e., God forbid)
Example: "If this computer does not work, absit omen, we will be in big trouble."

Ab uno disce omnes - From one example, learn all. (Virgil)
Example: "There are cases where just from a single example, all can learn a general truth, therefore ab uno disce omnes."

A capite ad calcem - From head to heel (totally, entirely)
Example: "This lady is in red a capite ad calcem."

Ac etiam - And also
Example: "We had to solve many cases ac etiam to help some other teams."

Ad damnum - To the damages (i.e., amount demanded).
Example: "There were some damages to the car and ad damnum was $1000."

Adde parvum parvo magnus acervus erit (Ovid) - Add a little to a little and there will be a great heap

Example: "We all notice from experience that if you adde parvum parvo magnus acervus erit."

Additur - Let it be increased
Example: "This team decided to spend for the new computer the amount of $500, but the manager said additur by $200."

Adesse - To be present
Example: "When the conference will begin they want adesse."

Ad finem fidelis - Faithful to the end
Example: "The supporters of this team were ad finem fidelis."

Ad gustum - To one's taste
Example: "When the group went to a restaurant, everyone ordered ad gustum."

Adhibendus - To be administered

Example: "The doctor recommended a certain medicine adhibendus."

Ad hoc - For this; for a specific occasion; impromptu
Example: "To improve the quality, a manager was selected ad hoc."

Ad hunc locum - At this place
Example: "Our new house will be built ad hunc locum."

Ad idem - To the same point
Example: "The two engineers finally arrived ad idem regarding the solution for a technical problem."

Ad instar – According to; like
Example: "The engineer was appointed as manager, ad instar the rules of the company."

Ad instar omnium - In the likeness of all
Example: "The portret of the team was ad instar omnium."

Adiuvante Deo labor proficit - With God's help, work prospers.
Example: "An old man was looking at the efforts after an earthquake and said Adiuvante Deo labor proficit."

Ad libitum (ad lib) - At pleasure; extemporaneously or freely
Example: "This musical piece has an ad libitum part, for improvisations.

Ad litteram - To the letter (i.e., precisely)
Example: "Many translations are required to be ad litteram."

Ad locum - At the place, at a specific location
    Example: "We plan this building to be ad locum."

Ad manum - At hand (i.e., ready and prepared)
    Example: "This consultant is ad manum to provide necessary services."

Ad meliora vertamur - Let us turn to better things
    Example: "An old man observed a group of young people wasting their time with inutile controversies, and kindly told them ad meliora vertamur."

Ad misericordiam - To pity (i.e., appealing to mercy)
    Example: "Not being able to get an approval for his project, the contractor tried ad misericordiam arguments."

Ad modum - In the manner of; consistent with
    Example: "This young poet tries to write ad modum Horace."

Ad nauseam - To the point of sickness; to nausea: to the point of being disgusted
    Example: "Sometime politicians repeat a certain topic ad nauseam."

Ad personal - To the person; relating to the individual
    Example: "This company produces ad personal items."

Ad populum - To the people
    Example: "All politicians address ad populum, and say what the people want to hear."

Ad quod damnum - To what damage
    Example: "When there is an accident, there are discussions about the amount to be paid ad quod damnum."

Ad referendum - For reference; for further consideration
Example: "This agreement is ad referendum, and needs to be approved by a manager."

Ad rem - To the point; relevant to the present matter
Example: "We have an important issue here, and let's have the discussions ad rem."

Ad saturatum - To saturation
Example: "They discussed this subject ad saturatum."

Adsum - I am present; to be present
Example: "An important decision is discussed at this meeting and adsum."

Ad summam - In short; in a word
Example: "After the concert many different comments appeared, but the conclusion was, ad summam, good."

Adsummum - To the highest point
Example: "Working with dedication on many projects, this team arrived adsummum."

Ad unguem - To the fingernail (i.e., with great precision)
Example: "The expert tested the smoothness of a telescopic mirror and said with satisfaction: it is ad unguem."

Ad unum omnes - All to one; in a unanimous fashion
Example: "After many discussions, the decision was adopted ad unum omnes."

Ad usum - According to custom; to usage

Example: "If a company has a subsidiary in another country, that subsidiary has to operate ad usum for that country."

Ad utrumque paratus (Virgil) - Ready for both; prepared for either alternative
Example: "A good emergency team is ad utrumque paratus."

Ad valorem - According to value
Example: "Taxes on property are assessed ad valorem of that property."

Ad verecundiam - Appeal to respect or modesty in an argument
Example: "In his presentation, the consultant made an ad verecundiam in order to justify his request."

Adversus - Against; contrary to
Example: "He had a point of view adversus the opinion of his colleague."

Aequabiliter et diligenter - Equably and diligently
Example: "The conference was managed aequabiliter et diligenter."

Afflatus montium - Mountain air

Example: "When they visited Utah and Switzerland, they could feel the pleasant afflatus montium."

A fortiori - With even stronger reason; all the more
Example: "This project was completed, therefore, a fortiori, a particular task from the project was also completed.

Age quod agis - Do what you are doing (i.e., pay attention to what you are doing)
Example: "In order to have a work of good quality, it is important to age quod agis."

Agita - Shake or stir
Example: "It is recommended to agita many juices before you drink them."

A latere - From the side; with confidence
Example: "This project has a task a latere, but it is important."

Alia tentanda via est - Another way must be tried
Example: "When a certain method for solving a problem is not successful, alia tentanda via est."

Alimenta - Means of support (i.e., food, clothing, shelter)
Example: "A welfare program for orphans first needs alimenta."

Alio intuitu - From another point of view
Example: "After the consultant gave an explanation of the project, the manager approached the project alio intuitu."

Alter ego - One's second self; other I

Example: "Sometimes I have debates with myself on an issue, and it looks like a debate between me and my alter ego."

Alter idem - Another of the same kind; second self
Example: "For their project they had a powerful computer, but they needed alter idem."

Alternis diebus - Every other day
Example: "The engineer had access to some sophisticated equipment alternis diebus."

Alternis horis - Every other hour
Example: "For a short period of time, the child had to take some medications alternis horis."

Alternis noctibus – On alternate nights
Example: "For security reason, the passwords had to be changed alternis noctibus."

Alterum alterius auxilio eget – Each needs the help of the other
Example: "To solve a complicated technical emergency, alterum alterius auxilio eget."

Balneum - Bath
Example: "The very popular balneum had been appreciated by Romans starting before 250 BC."

Cacoethes - Irresistible urge to do something inadvisable
Example: "This worker has a cacoethes for smoking."

Divide et impera - Divide and rule *or* Divide and conquer *or* Divide in order to conquer

Example: "In the fight against the growth of the health care costs, a good idea is to use the Roman method divide et impera."

Durate et vosmet rebus servate secundis - Carry on and preserve yourselves for better times. (Virgil)
Example: "The team was working hard on a difficult project, and the manager told them durate et vosmet rebus servate secundis."

Bis vincit qui se vincit in victoria - He conquers twice who conquers himself in victory. (Publius Syrus)
Example: "In sport, the victorious team was kind with the defeated one, because bis vincit qui se vincit in victoria."

Dimidium facti, qui coepit habet - He who has begun is half done. (Horace)
Example: "It is important to start well a project, because dimidium facti, qui coepit habet."

Faber est suae quisque fortunae (Appius Claudius Caecus) - Every man is the maker of his own fortune.
Example: "The professor emphasized the importance of self-responsibility, because faber est suae quisque fortunae."

Idem - The same
Example: "The presenter gave the name of a book at beginning, then later, referring to this book, said: compare idem."

Id est - That is
Example: "The engineer explained this project in detail, id est he gave all the tasks which need to be performed."

Ipso facto - By the fact itself
    Example: "Doing a bad product, the worker was condemned ipso facto."

Mirabile dictu - Wonderful to tell
    Example: "We were visiting Rome, and, mirabile dictum, the Trajan's column, erected in 113 AD, appears before us."

Mirabile visu - Wonderful to see
    Example: "It is always mirabile visu the progress of these children at school."

Meo periculo - At my own risk
    Example: "I decided, meo periculo, to start a project, which everybody was saying that cannot be done."

Nil desperandum - Never despair
    Example: "When the students are with their professor of mathematics, they nil desperandum."

Nota bene - Note well
Example: "I explain here some details of our work, and, nota bene, there are special security issues."

Noli intrare - Do not enter; keep out
Example: "There was a special laboratory in the company, with a clear sign on the door: noli intrare."

Noli perturbare - Do not disturb
Example: "A beautiful classical music could be heard from a music class, and on the door was a sign: Noli perturbare."

Nullo modo - No way
Example: "Maybe we can postpone this work, somebody said; nullo modo, responded the manager."

Post mortem - After death
Example: "There are many writers and composers who became famous only post mortem."

Prima facie - On the first view
Example: "This software project, prima facie, seemed easy, but shortly it was noticed that there are many difficulties."

Primus inter pares - First among equals
Example: "There were several good engineers in this company, but Michael was primus inter pares."

Sine die - Without a day; indefinitely
Explanation: It is originally from the old common law texts, where it indicates that a final, dispositive order has been made in a case. In modern legal context, it means there is nothing left for the court to do, so no date for further proceedings is set.

Example: "Our meeting was postponed sine die."

Sine qua non - Without which it could not be; essential
Example: "A sine qua non condition for happiness is morality."

Status quo - The state in which things are now; the existing state of affairs
Example: "In many countries the governments want to preserve the status quo, but the people want changes for better living conditions."

Candor dat viribus alas - Candor gives wings to strength
Example: "After many years of experience, he noticed that candor dat viribus alas."

Dum vita est spes est - While there is life, there is hope
Example: "Sometimes it appears that there is no hope, but dum vita est spes est."

Dum spiro, spero - While I breathe, I hope
Example: "In the middle of great difficulties, I always remember that dum spiro, spero."

Amor vincit omnia (Virgil) - Love conquers all
Example: "It is an eternal truth that amor vincit omnia."

Cras amet qui nunquam amavit; quique amavit, cras amet - May he love tomorrow who has never loved before; and may he who has loved, love tomorrow as well
Example: "A beautiful homage to the importance of love is this: cras amet qui nunquam amavit; quique amavit, cras amet."

Quid novi? - What's new?

Example: "When the manager came back, he asked: quid novi?"

Volens nolens - Whether you like it or not
Explanation: It is also used in the form **Nolens volens** – Unwilling, willing. That is, "whether unwillingly or willingly". Sometimes expressed **aut nolens aut volens** or **nolentis volentis**. It is similar to willy-nilly, though that word is derived from Old English will-he nil-he ([whether] he will or [whether] he will not).
Example: "You received this task, and, volens nolens, you have to do it."

Vade in pace - Go in peace (one of the Roman "goodbye" expressions)
Example: "After a good meeting, we said to each other vade in pace."

Vice versa - The other way around; the terms being reversed
Example: "When law becomes bad, morals are bad, and vice versa."

Chapter II. 6 - Law

Absens haeres non erit - The absent one will not be beneficiary
    Example: "Mark was not present at the discussions, therefore we'll apply the rule absens haeres non erit."

Abusus non tollit usum - Abuse does not remove use
    Example: "If someone drink too much beer, it does not mean to make beer illegal, because abusus non tollit usum."

Absolvo - I absolve; I acquit
    Example: "After a short deliberation about a minor error of a student, the professor said absolvo."

Absque ulla nota - Without any marks
    Example: "After a team analyzed a good proposal, they approved it absque ulla nota."

Accedas ad curiam - You may approach the court
> *Example:* "When you are ready, accedas ad curiam."

Lex non distinguitur nos non distinguere debemus - The law does not distinguish and so we ought not distinguish.
> *Example*: "There are places where the law is not the same for all, and we have to reiterate that lex non distinguitur nos non distinguere debemus."

Legum servi sumus ut liberi esse possimus (Cicero) - We are slaves of the law so that that we may be free.
> *Example:* "If only one is free and the others are not – this is dictatorship. We can have freedom for everybody, if we all comply with the law, therefore: legum servi sumus ut liberi esse possimus."

Accipiunt leges, populus quibus legibus ex lex (Lucilius) - They consent to laws, which place people outside the law.
> *Example:* "A sign of dictatorship is when accipiunt leges, populus quibus legibus ex lex."

Aes alienum - Money belonging to another; a debt
> *Example:* "The company discovered that an important amount of money was actually aes alienum."

Actus Dei - Act of God
> *Example:* "When there is actus Dei, all people help."

Aequitas sequitur legem - Equity follows the law
> *Example:* "Impartiality is essential in applying the law, and for this we have aequitas sequitur legem."

Contra ius commune - Against common law
> *Example:* "This worker did something which was contra ius commune."

De jure (de iure) – Concerning the law; legally
  Example: "This company has fulfilled its legal requirements, therefore it is a De Jure Company."

Culpam poena premit comes (Horace) - Punishment follows closely behind crime's heels
  Example: "It is good for everybody to know that culpam poena premit comes."

Culpae poenae par esto - Let the punishment fit the crime
  Example: "This is what all the good people are saying for thousands of years: culpae poenae par esto."

Culpa lata - Gross fault
  Example: "This person has committed a culpa lata and he will be punished."

Culpa levis - Ordinary negligence
  Example: "Being a culpa levis for this young man, he will be sent for more training and education."

Consensus facit legem - Consent makes the law
  Example: "If there is consent about a contract between two parties, then the contract becomes law, because consensus facit legem."

Corruptissima re publica plurimae leges (Publius Cornelius Tacitus) - In a very corrupt state are the most laws
  Example: "When there is much corruption, then more laws are needed to try to eliminate different types of corruption, therefore corruptissima re publica plurimae leges."

De minimis non curat lex - The law does not concern itself with trifles

Example: "When somebody does a minor legal mistake, no court intervention is necessary, because de minimis non curat lex."

Durum hoc est sed ita lex scripta est - This is harsh, but the law is written.
Example: "Sometimes the punishment appears to be hard, but they say durum hoc est sed ita lex scripta est."

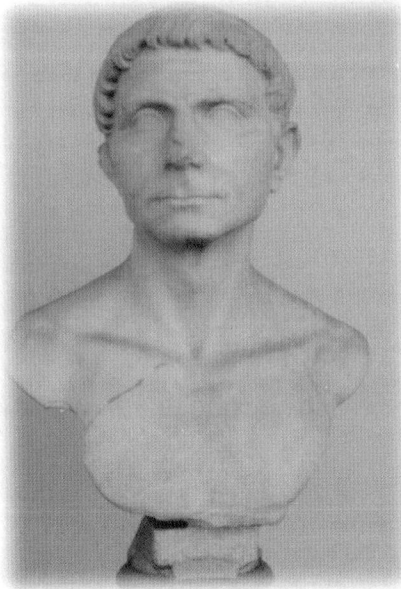

Dura lex sed lex -The law is harsh, but it is the law
Example: "Some may not like a severe punishment, but dura lex sed lex."

Contra ius gentium - Against the law of nations
Example: "In international business it is important not to act contra ius gentium."

Ad iudicium - To judgment; to common sense.

Example: "When making a decision, let's not forget to be ad iudicium."

Mea culpa - My fault
Example: "When you make a mistake, simply say mea culpa."

Nemo iudex in causa sua - No man shall be a judge in his own cause
Explanation: Legal principle that no individual can preside over a hearing in which he holds a specific interest or bias.
Example: "If you are in dispute with another person, you cannot be a judge in this dispute, because nemo iudex in causa sua."

Chapter II. 7 - Miscellanea

Abiit, excessit, evasit, erupit (Cicero) - He has departed, absconded, escaped, disappeared
    Example: "When you see that a man wants to really go away, you can say abiit, excessit, evasit, erupit."

Ab uno ad omnes - From one to all
    Example: "When somebody has a good idea and all the others agree with that idea, we say ab uno ad omnes."

Ad arbitrium - At will; arbitrarily; at pleasure
    Example: "Only dictators can act ad arbitrium."

Ad captandum - For the sake of pleasing
    Example: "Many politicians say certain things just ad captandum."

Ad clerum - To the clergy

Example: "When a church leader wants to address only to the clergy, he says ad clerum."

Ad crumenam - To the purse. (i.e., appealing to self-interest)
Example: "Many salesmen continuously speak ad crumenam."

Ad effectum – To the effect
Example: "The engineer explained this technical process ad effectum."

Adeste Fideles - O, come, all ye faithful
Example: "It is so beautiful this hymn Adeste Fideles."

Ad eundem gradum - To the same degree (i.e., equal blame or praise).
Example: "This student from a local university asked to be admitted ad eundem gradum to another university."

Ad extra - To the outside
Example: "We usually talk to our team, but occasionally we need to address ad extra."

Ad fidem - To faith
Example: "Many apostolic letters refer ad fidem."

Ad filum viae - To the center of the road
Example: "The local Land Registry applies the principle of ad filum viae to determine the ownership of the land."

Ad hanc vocem - To this word

Example: "Mark noted that these words appear to be related ad hanc vocem."

Ad quem - To or for whom; to or for which.
Example: "The managed set a day ad quem this project must be finished."

Adversus solem ne loquitor - Don't speak against the Sun (i.e., an obvious fact)
Example: "When somebody tries to explain obvious things, just say adversus solem ne loquitor."

Aedificatum - That which is built
Example: "This new building here looks like aedificatum over there."

Aes triplex (Horace) - Triple bronze; a strong defense
Example: "This military unit has aes triplex."

Afflatus (Cicero) - Breath; breeze; poetic inspiration.
Example: "In solving some difficult problems you need a lot of hard work, but also some afflatus."

A fronte praecipitium a tergo lupi - a precipice in front and wolves behind (between a rock and a hard place)
Example: "When you find yourself in a situation like with a fronte praecipitium a tergo lupi, do not despair and ask for help."

Agnosco veteris vestigia flammae (Virgil) - I recognize the signs of the old flame
Example: "This man tells his wife about his love for her: agnosco veteris vestigia flammae."

Albo lapillo notare diem - To mark the day with a white stone.

Example: "This is a happy day, therefore we want albo lapillo notare diem."

Albus – White
Example: "The albus snow is all over the land."

Liber albus - White book
Example: "There is a Liber albus of the City of London."

Alere flammam (Ovid) - To feed the flames
Example: "It is important alere flammam of liberty and hard work ubiquitously."

Alias – An assumed name; otherwise; at another time.
Example: "This author uses an alias for his books of poetry."

Alias dictus – Otherwise called, an assumed name; also known as, aka.
Example: "Richard, alias dictus Bobby, was a good chemist."

Alibi – Elsewhere
Example: "He used an alibi escuse, not to be blamed for an accident."

Alieni generis - Of a different class
Example: "The current project is alieni generis compared to the previous project."

Alienum est omne quicquid optando evenit - What we obtain by asking is not really ours
Example: "If you receive something by asking, remember that alienum est omne quicquid optando evenit."

Aliquid - Something; somewhat
   Example: "Observing aliquid abnormal on the computer screen, he asked a specialist for help."

Aliunde - From another source; from outside; from elsewhere
   Example: "This information came aliunde and it is not reliable."

Alterum tantum - As much again; twice as much
   Example: "Sometimes fines are alterum tantum in places where there is work in progress."

Amari aliquid - Something bitter; a touch of bitterness
   Example: "On a very sweet chocolate it is nice to add amari aliquid."

Ambigendi locus - Room for doubt

Example: "When they examined all the details of that problem, there was plenty of ambigendi locus."

Hic et ubique - Here and everywhere
Example: "All the scientific laws are valic hic et ubique."

Ignis internum - The fire within
Example: "For many artists, ignis internum is essential for creating new works.

Meum et tuum - Mine and tine
Example: "Classical works, which are available for all, are meum et tuum."

Noli me tangere - Don't touch me; touch me not
Example: "An aristocratic lady addressed to an young man with the classical noli me tangere."

Sententiae latinae – Latin maxims
Example: "It is very beneficial and pleasant to often use sententiae latinae."

Chapter II. 8 – Science

A caelo usque ad centrum - From the sky to the center of the earth
  Example: "In the Roman times, an owner owned everything a caelo usque ad centrum, but these days we have airplanes, oil exploration under your house, etc."

Ad absurdum - To the absurd
  Example: "In mathematics, the method of proof by reductio ad absurdum is very useful and important."

Ad amussim - According to a rule (i.e., with precision, accurately)
  Example: "This software development project was done ad amussim."

Ad astra - To the starts
  Example: "We should make every effort to explore other planets, and to go ad astra."

Ad ignorantiam - To ignorance [of the facts of an argument]
  Example: "He cannot use an appeal ad ignorantiam, because he knew all the facts of this problem."

Aequales - Equal parts
  Example: "The students are working on a problem to divide a circle in 7 aequales."

Aequilibrium indifferentiae - State of exact balance between two actions
  Example: "There are many studies in physics related to the aequilibrium indifferentiae."

Aliquant - An uneven part of the whole
Example: "In mathematics, when a number n1 is not a divisor of another number n2, we say n1 is an aliquant part of n2, e.g. 7 is an aliquant part of 19."

A maximis ad minima - From the maximum to the minimum
Example: "Whatever is the intensity of your work, a maximis ad minima, always pay attention to quality."

Natura valde simplex est et sibi consona (Newton) - Nature is exceedingly simple and harmonious with itself
Example: "The nature is extremely complex, but seen from a particular point of view, like Newton's, natura valde simplex est et sibi consona."

Naturam expellas furca, tamen usque recurret (Horace) - Nature can be expelled with a fork, but nevertheless always returns

Example: "When you take the basic nature of everything into account you notice that naturam expellas furca, tamen usque recurret."

Natura abhorret a vacuo - Nature abhors a vacuum.
    Example: "Before the discovery of the atmospheric pressure, the pseudo-explanation, for why a liquid will climb up a tube to fill a vacuum, was natura abhorret a vacuo.

Sapiens nihil affirmat quod non probat - A wise man states as true nothing he does not prove
    Example: "Proving is the fundamental rule of science, therefore sapiens nihil affirmat quod non probat."

Tera incognita - An unknown land
    Example: "There are still parts of the Earth which are tera incognita."

Chapter II. 9 - History

Actum est de re publica - It is all over with the republic
  Example: "When the people of a country do not pay enough attention to the military defense, an enemy will attack and occupy the country, and then actum est de re publica."

A cuspide corona - From the spear a crown.
  Example: "Many times in the past, the kings got their crowns by spears and wars, therefore a cuspide corona."

Ad baculum - To the stick (i.e., appeal to force, not reason)
  Example: "Unfortunately there are still countries where the main argument is ad baculum."

Ad captandum vulgus – To capture the crowd
  Example: "Many things are done in this world just ad captandum vulgus."

A Deo et rege - From God and the king
  Example: "The kings used the expression a Deo et rege to impose their will on the people."

Ad perpetuam rei memoriam - For the perpetual remembrance of the thing
  Example: "On some official documents of the church it is written ad perpetuam rei memoriam."

Adscriptus glebae - Attached to the soil; a serf
  Example: "In feudal days, like in Russia until 1861, a laborer, which was adscriptus glebae, could be sold with the land."

Alea iacta est - The die is cast

Example: "Julius Caesar, having made the decision to cross the river Rubicon in January 10, 49 BC, to begin a war against Pompey, said: alea iacta est."

Salus populi suprema lex esto (Cicero) - The welfare of the people is to be the highest law

Semper fidelis - Always faithful
Example: "The official motto from 1883 and the marching song of the United States Marine Corps is Semper Fidelis."

Semper paratus - Always ready
Example: "The official motto and the marching song of the United States Coast Guard is Semper Paratus."

Si vis pacem, para bellum (Publius Flavius Vegetius Renatus) - If you want peace, prepare for war

SPQR - Senatus Populusque Romanus - The Senate and the People of Rome
SPQR was the official name of the Roman Republic. "SPQR" was carried on battle standards by the Roman legions. In addition to being an ancient Roman motto, it remains the motto of the modern city of Rome.

Veni vidi vici - I came, I saw, I conquered

    Example: "In 47 B.C. Julius Caesar sent the laconic dispatch veni vidi vici to the Senate, regarding his victory over Pharnaces, king of Pontus."

Vi et armis - By force and arms

    Example: "When somebody tries to persuade vi et armis, it may be necessary to respond in the same way."

Chapter II. 10 - Medical

Absente febre – In the absence of fever
Example: "His influenza developed absente febre."

Ad partes dolentes - To the painful parts
Example: "Special medication was applied ad partes dolentes."

Adstante febre - When fever is present
Example: "In this case, a different medical instruction is given adstante febre."

Ad usum externum - For external use
Example: "There are many medicines which are only ad usum externum."

Ad vivum - To the life
Example: "The best ad vivum anesthesiology can be found in many good hospitals."

Aeger - Sick; ill
Example: "In British universities the students use aeger as a medical excuse."

Aegrescit medendo (Virgil) - The disease worsens with the treatment
Example: "Until recently, the medical treatment was not very scientific, and, sometimes, aegrescit medendo."

Aegri somnia vana (Virgil) - A sick man's dream; hallucination
Example: "When a patient has high fever, a consequence could be aegri somnia vana."

Aegrotat - He is sick

    Example: "In British universities, if some students are too sick to pass an examination, then each obtains an aegrotat."

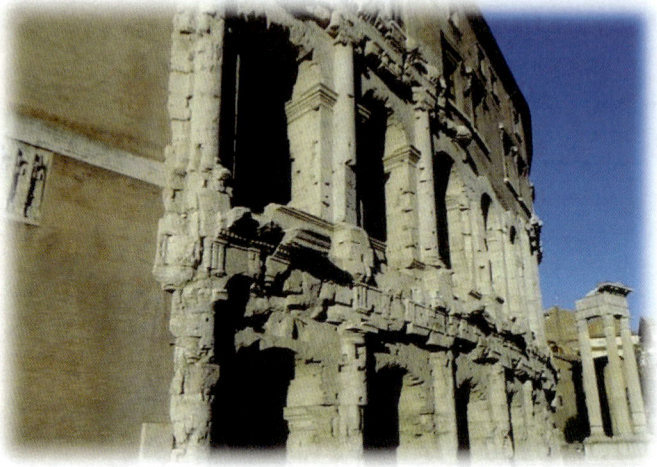

Aequam servare mentem (Horace) - To preserve a calm mind; equanimity

    Example: "In difficult situations it is imperative aequam servare mentem."

Aequam memento rebus in arduis servare mentem (Horace) - Remember to maintain a calm mind while doing difficult tasks

    Example: "The manager used to tell his team: aequam memento rebus in arduis servare mentem."

Aequanimitas - With composure; with equanimity; imperturbability

    Example: "One of the most important requirements for physicians is aequanimitas."

Aequo animo - With a calm mind; with equanimity
    Example: "I observed him working, in very stressful situations, aequo animo."

Aeternum servans sub pectore vulnus (Virgil) - Nursing an everlasting wound within the breast
    Example: "When there is a big disappointment, we feel like aeternum servans sub pectore vulnus."

Aggrediente febre - When the fever increases
    Example: "In this case, there are special medical procedures aggrediente febre."

Agita nate sumendum - Shake before taking
    Example: "On many bottles with liquid medicines it is written agita nate sumendum."

Alterum non laedere - Not to injure other
    Example: "A very important rule in any human activity is alterum non laedere."

Mens sana in corpore sano (Juvenal) - A sound mind in a sound body
    Example: "It is a perpetual desire for everybody to have mens sana in corpore sano."

Non compos mentis - Not of sound mind
    Example: "The medical doctors have to determine if a person is non compos mentis."

Primum non nocere - Above all do no harm; first do not harm
    Example: "All the medical doctors have to take the Hippocratic Oath, which contains, as a fundamental medical dictum, primum non nocere."

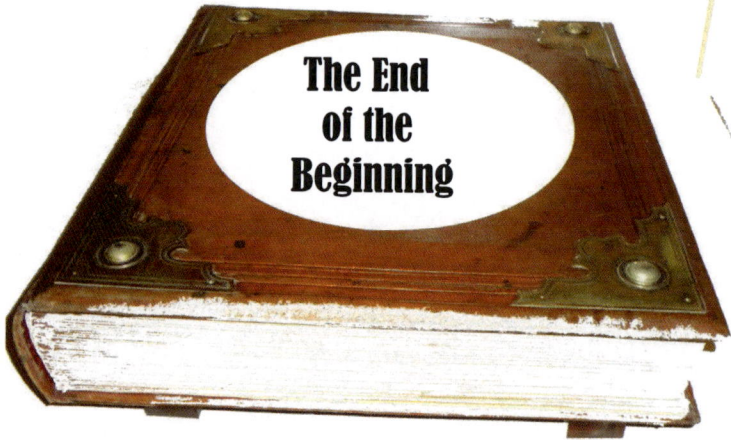

The End
of the
Beginning

Made in the USA
Charleston, SC
29 February 2012